To

Iain Sinclair

Around the M60

Manchester's Orbital Motorway

by Matthew Hyde, Aidan O'Rourke & Peter Portland

Published by AMCD (Publishers) Limited, PO Box 182, Altrincham, Cheshire,
WA16 9UA England

Contact: web@amcd.co.uk

ISBN: 1897762305

First Published: 2004

Copyright of individual images and photographs is as attributed at the end of the text.

Design by: Pocknell Studio

Contents:

Left: Head of an Unknown
Goddess. This stone head of
adorns the north facade of
Abney Hall at Cheadle.

Above: Junction 1 at dusk in the rain. Looking west along the M60 Motorway (formerly the M63) at Cheadle Heath at dusk in torrential rain. Sign points left to Cheadle (A34) and straight on to Ring Road (W and N), M62, M61, Manchester Airport, M56 and M6.

Manchesters's M60 Motorway: *A Personal Introduction* - I am roughly the same age as Britains Motorway sytem, born in 1958, the year the M1 and the M6 Preston By-pass were opened. The M62 Eccles By-pass, now part of the M60 Motorway, was opened when I was one and a half; the renamed M60 Motorway was only completed on Monday, October 30th 2000, when I was forty two.

Born in Stockport, just south of where the M60 passes today, I've seen the motorways grow from pristine isolated sections within an ageing landscape, to what they are today, the backbone of the regional and national road transport system.

As a child I rode across the old Barton Bridge on Bullocks coach excursions to Blackpool. On the bus to London my dad and I admired the newly constructed M6 with its curved concrete bridges, the neat lane lines, the sky-blue signs whose lettering seemed the epitome of modernity. At night the brightly-lit motorway snaking through the urban landscape was like a highway into the future – my future. I dreamed of when I would be 17 and able to apply for my provisional driving licence, learn to drive and eventually cruise the motorway in my sister's Austin 1100. I looked at construction work on the M63 near Cheadle (again now part of the M60) and I whispered to myself 'When this motorway is completed, I'll have my driving licence'.

The urban landscape I remember as a child was very different to the one we see today. Grimy factories with chimneys, railway lines blackened by soot from the steam trains; and roads mostly a legacy from

earlier centuries – narrow, dimly lit by bluish-green street lamps; murky canals covered with oil slicks and floating debris. By comparison, the pristine new motorway was a liberating experience. There were no speed limits in the early days and not much traffic – a 100 mph 'ton-up' was still possible. Inspired by science-fiction films, I imagined the motorways of the future criss-crossing Manchester, used by neat lines of cars, all moving smoothly at the same speed, like a model railway.

The M60 Motorway of today is a different story – often congested with endless traffic jams, pounded incessantly by super-juggernauts, buses and cars, the once spotless surface now sullied by exhaust fumes, skid marks, road debris or road kill, and the remains of temporary lane lines. The motorway – statistically the safest type of road – can be a place of danger, of death. I've seen the flashing lights, traffic cones, mangled metal and sometimes bodies on the road.

The M60 Motorway has now become a part of our lives, something most people hardly give a second thought to. But to me the M60 Motorway is much more than just a means of getting from A to B. It's a defining symbol of the age we live in, as well as an amazing feat of civil engineering, which ought to rank with the achievements of Britain's Victorian engineers. It's an all-dominating element of the newly-recreated urban landscape. It has redefined how we work, play, shop and travel, and it has

Above: Stockport Railway Viaduct. View from above Hollywood park looking east towards the stockport railway viaduct. On the right are Stockport council flats built in the 1960's.

The M60 (Manchester Orbital) and the M25 (London Orbital):

	M25	M60
Length - miles (km)	117 (187)	35 (56)
Building Period	1975 - Dartford Tunnel Approach, to 1986	1957 - Eccles Bypass to 2000
Cost (current prices)	£1693mn (est.)	£1150mn (est.)
Cost (£) per mile	£14.5mn (est.)	£32.9mn (est)
Widening (£) per mile	£19.7mn (Jc. 12-15)	£24.4mn (Jcn. 5-8)
Annual Maintenance	£10.5mn (est.)	£3.1mn (est.)
Number of Junctions	32 (including 21A)	27
Number of Bridges over (including foot bridges)	264	68
Avereage distance between junctions	3.7 (6.6km)	1.3 (2.1km)
Service Stations	3	None

created new relationships between the places it links and with the places it passes by.

As we whizz by at 70 mph – or more – we often forget what's beyond the hard shoulder. Accessible from the motorway, there's a world of places to explore – places which often were previously difficult to get to. A few feet away from the concrete highway and its screaming traffic there are timeless spots with an air of tranquility – if you could only shut out the traffic noise. Churches, ponds, parks, houses, tourist attractions, town centres and shopping precincts – a selection of them are featured here.

I'm also fascinated by the path taken by the motorway, and its remarkable intersections, geometrical collisions and incidences with older forms of transport and with geographical features such as rivers and county boundaries. The myriad of statistics, quirky facts and interesting anecdotes relating to the motorway are also an education in themselves. Here they are, for your delectation.

The M60 is a prime example of the ultimate superhighway, a high-speed road with flyovers, bridges and underpasses of the type which we in the UK call a motorway. The M60 is an orbital motorway, enclosing 100 square miles of the inner part of the industrial conurbation in north west England known as Manchester – one of the early seedbeds of the industrial revolution. Its population catchment area is perhaps some three million people. With its irregular, squashed oval shape and pointed top at Prestwich, the M60 Motorway around Manchester appears logical and easy to understand and visualise. And yet this gargantuan beltway came about in an unplanned way, cobbled together from sections of existing motorway.

The oldest stretch of the M60 is from Chester Road (A56) in the south west to Eccles Road (A57) in the west, incorporating the Barton High Level Bridge.

This was the first stretch of urban motorway to be built in the UK. Opened in 1959 as the M62, and known more commonly as the Eccles By-pass, it was designed to take traffic around Trafford Park Industrial Estate, linking the northern side of the Manchester Ship Canal in Lancashire with the main A56 road south west of Manchester bordering on Cheshire. Since then the Eccles By-pass has been widened and rebuilt, but that first section of motorway retains a place in history.

The newest stretch of the M60 is one of the most advanced sections of motorway ever built. It was opened in autumn 2000 – four years late, and links the Denton intersection (Junction 24) with Middleton (Junction 18). It immediately took 50,000 cars off Manchester's other roads, but increased flows along the Motorway by an enormous 27% from new 'induced trips' or merely 're-routing' in the planners' jargon. With its sophisticated bridges, embankments and junction layouts, the M60 here represents state-of-the-art motorway design. And yet this culmination of engineering technology has a major flaw: during heavy rain it is prone to flooding – investigations have been carried out, questions asked in the House of Commons, but still the engineers don't know quite why. Maybe the problem has something to do with the fact that one of the three Audenshaw reservoirs was drained and removed to make way for the Motorway. As if to acknowledge this superior force of the elements, permanent signs have been erected with the warning 'Road liable to flooding'!

Other sections of the motorway were built in separate construction phases, bearing the designations M61, M62, and M63. The north western portion forms part of the M62 from Liverpool to Hull. Since re-designation to the M60, the M62 is now split into two sections. The M60 southern stretch from Stockport to Stretford was built in the 1980s and named the M63. The section from Portwood to the east of Stockport to Denton in the east came about in the early 1990s. It incorporates some unique junction layouts, including one of the few slip roads on British motorways to merge coming from the offside lane – an arrangement more common on American Interstate Highways, and here a cause of accidents.

All around the M60 there are remarkable and mostly unsung feats of engineering – huge embankments formed from earth dug out of vast holes in the ground, now artificial lakes; bridges spanning lesser roads, railways or canals – often two at a time. Supreme here is the gigantic Barton Bridge with its panoramic views of the Ship Canal and the Trafford Centre.

Equally impressive is the claustrophobic section of the M60 through Stockport, which required extensive drilling and excavation work of the red sandstone, obscuring a whole part of the town and a former railway line and station. The M60 is still too contemporary a product – it is taken for granted – but this marvel of civil engineering deserves to be admired as much as that other great engineering feat of the Victorians which it pierces, the Stockport Railway Viaduct over the River Mersey. First built in 1839, with its 27 arches and 11 million red bricks, it is one of the largest viaducts in Europe. Unsung and uncelebrated, it carries the railway south, through the Midlands to London.

The M60 Motorway is then a microcosm of the story of Britain's motorways, containing sections built during every decade since the 1950s. The M60 is however more a haphazard creation, emerging over a period of 40 years, than a carefully planned and constructed highway. It has serious flaws in the way it handles traffic flow. Many junctions can only be accessed in one direction, and at some you may end up doing a large detour if you don't know exactly where to come on and off. For example, to join the motorway at Junction 2 at Kingsway you must make

a one mile detour via Sharston to access the main motorway going north west. And the biggest flaw can be found at the northerly tip of the oval, near the village of Simister. Here, eight-lane stretches of what were two and are now three motorways (M66, M60 and the M62) intersect roughly at right angles. Access from one to the other is via that rare beast, a motorway roundabout controlled that device which defeats the whole point of a motorway – namely traffic lights.

To get from the M60 north west section (formerly M62) onto the north east section (formerly M66), you have to weave your way around the traffic lights, a roundabout, slip roads and lanes before you are back onto the motorway you've just left. Why is this? Because the legislators and the planners changed their minds!

Despite these blemishes, the M60 Motorway has redefined all locations and made them more accessible. Its path, across the roads, railway lines, canals, air lanes and geographical features it intersects, is a journey of discovery in itself. There are hidden geographical reasons for every bend, every knick, every curve and every junction layout (why the planners planned it so, is the most mysterious of all). Come then, on a journey round Manchester's orbital motorway, the M60 – a journey through time, a journey from the smoky past into a hazy future. **AOR**

Above: Three Rivers Meet.
Goyt, Thame and Mersey:
The motorway passes over the
confluence of the Goyt (near side)
and the Tame (flowing from the
right) which marks the start of
the River Mersey.

14

Stockport Severed - This is the start of the end of the M60 numbering system, and Stockport is the only major town centre the M60 Motorway actually passes through. Stockport town proper, lying at the south east of the motorway, presents a remarkable confluence of transport routes and geographical lines – an ancient boundary runs along the river Mersey, while the disused Tiviot Dale railway line, the Manchester Airport approach path and now the M60, all come together at Stockport town centre.

Is it pure co-incidence that at this point we have a confluence of river, rail, water and aerial routes, combined with an ancient geographical boundary? It's certainly significant, and places Stockport at a remarkable and providential location.

Let's look back over a thousand years, when the River Mersey – Anglo Saxon for 'boundary river' – passed through a valley with sandstone cliffs on either side, and continued its meandering path westwards towards the Irish Sea. The boundary which this river marked was between the ancient warring kingdoms of Mercia to the south, and Northumbria to the north. The partly Welsh place name Cheadle shows straggling Britons caught in the middle. The ford at the base of the sandstone cliff was one of the few crossing points for the Mersey. To the south of the River, on the hill above the ford, there was a castle, long since disappeared. The settlement which built up

around the castle became known as Stopford, later Stockport.

As the ancient kingdoms of England gave way to the counties, the River Mersey came to mark the boundary between the twin county palatines of Lancashire to the north, and Cheshire to the south. Both counties already existed before the Domesday book. Stockport, standing on this ancient boundary, had a special significance. Though the river was never navigable, it defined the local area, and its motive power attracted cotton mills and warehouses, which were built along its length through the town. It later became a source of water for steam, and a conduit for effluent from the factories, bleachworks and dyeworks.

In 1839 a new landmark was added to the town – 'a stupendous viaduct of brick built construction' – part of the Manchester and Birmingham Railway. The viaduct was doubled in 1880, and was the largest brick-built structure in Europe. It still renders daily service, carrying state of the art Virgin Trains over the M60, railworks permitting.

So many changing transport routes and geographical lines passing through a small town centre is remarkable enough. But there is another transport route which passes across Stockport,

which is also highly significant. Manchester's Ringway Airport lies some six miles south west of Stockport. The site was chosen by Manchester Corporation in the 1930s in large part for its good climatic characteristics – much better than the older airfield at Barton (next to Junction 11).

The main runways at Ringway are laid out from north east to south west to align with prevailing winds, which blow mainly from the south west. This means that the north eastern approach path passes directly over Stockport town centre. From the Second World War onwards, planes of every type have passed around 1500 feet above the town, providing a spectacle for people on the ground, and striking views for people peering through the portholes of the planes. From the Lancasters and Dakotas of the 1950s to the Airbuses, Boeings and Advanced Turboprops of today, a daily flow of traffic moves towards the runways along this carriageway in the sky, over Stockport town centre, over the River Mersey, the railway viaduct, the M60 Motorway, and that strange beacon, the Blue Pyramid. **AOR**

Left: Stockport in the 1840s. Stockport Railway Viaduct over the River Mersey in the 1840s, looking Northeast. Mills and trains powered by steam and coal dominate this scene, but an older source of power can be seen in the windmill on Lancashire Hill at top left.

Above: M60 and Railway meet. A Virgin mainline train from London heads into Manchester over the Stockport viaduct. Below, the M60 heads west towards the Blue Pyramid. The Mersey is to the south.

Stockport Blue and Red - The Dominant Colour of Stockport for most of its history must have been ferruginous red: the mottles of sandstone where a distant precursor of the River Mersey laid down its shales. A colour respected in the Railway viaduct with its 27 arches and 11 million red bricks, costing £70,000 in 1839... (£4 mn. today). Actually a second viaduct was added to it in 1889, but the join is almost invisible.

Then in 1990 the Blue Pyramid sprang up. Blue as motorway signing. A building that appears in almost every set of directions for Stockport – "leave the M60 Motorway at the Blue Pyramid". A text over which future Egyptologists will puzzle. And the names are growing all around – 'Pyramid Garage', 'King's Reach' in 'The Valley of the Kings.'

Shapes change cities. Stockport has rebranded itself with a Pyramid of sharp edges of blue seen through red round-headed railway arches. Here the motorway slices the town in two piercing the railway viaduct, a vast wall of sandstone deposition on the right, the River Mersey away to the left and the Pyramid's dead reckoning straight ahead.

The Blue Pyramid was to have been one of three in the Valley of the Kings, lining up like the stars in Orion's Belt to guide the cargo cult airliners into Manchester Airport. One Pyramid proved enough. Cities from the middle ages onwards had buildings that extended outwards as they rose upwards. It required some kind of special vision of the late 20th century to create a structure that got smaller as it rose. A building with a vast atrium, blue leather furniture, blue engineering brick supports and

Above: Blue Pyramid in the rain.
Looking from the car park of
Petsmart and Office World. It is
a murky rainswept evening in
July 2003. Sodium vapour lamps
are reflected on the wet tarmac.
To the right of the pyramid is
St Matthew's Church, Edgeley.

above:The Blue Pyramid in fog –
000, as it appeared on the first
ay of the new millennium.
oking across Brinksway Bridge,
uilt in the 1830's and until 1994
e link between the A560 and
e M60 at Junction 1.

ght:The Blue Pyramid under
onstruction in 1990. The naked
amework of the Blue Pyramid
Stockport Junction 1 reveals
e simplicity of the design.
further two planned pyramids
this Valley of the Kings were
ver built.

vertigo-inducing outward-facing lifts. It stood empty over a long period – it did not prove easy to let – and the bankers to the project, the Co-op, decided to move in.

This is a place that Robert Owen, father of the Co-operative movement, grappling with the power of water and steam, dreaming his utopian visions in Scotland's New Lanark in the 1780s, could never have imagined: a place where money has been converted into electricity. This is a call centre for the Co-op's on-line banking, and the computer server farm for 'Smile,' its internet bank. Here, eager 18-20 year olds, preferably with reassuring Scots or Geordie accents, will unravel your account for you from 06:00 to 00:00. (It was 24 hour banking, but money, like people, preferred to sleep.)

Yet the structure is reassuringly simple: four concrete A frames laid slantingly together, with a lattice of steel to hold the sheets of blue glass – 1300 sheets, each the size of a double bed, made in Germany, £3,000 a throw. Seen from outside they are a deep electric blue (except for one, which the folklore has it, allows the Spirit of the Dead Clerk to exit the Pyramid) But inside there is no visible colour except a slight greyish tint. Outside the blue colour can in fact be varied at night by the use of lighting – the Blue Pyramid went pink for 'Breast Cancer Awareness Week.'

Can the Pyramid bear comparison with its nineteenth century banking counterparts on King Street in Manchester? They are solid heavy buildings, oozing banker's gravitas from their vermiculated facades, Athenian democracy and academia from their classic orders of columns. This Pyramid looks as though it is made of light, as though it is wirelessing down txt msgs through its apex. A pyramid as a bank is a new take on an old joke: 'Although bankers do not come to their business in fancy dress, they have, apparently,

no similar code for their buildings...' wrote one architect in 1915 of a similarly very odd bank building in central Manchester. But what is this in the foyer? Yes, a hole-in-the-wall cash machine, to convert electricity back into money – or at least into paper. Even call centre clerks need to draw breath and money.

To the south the River Mersey plunges satisfyingly and noisily into a steep defile. In these canyons until recently lived a Stockport hermit – alone in a sandstone cave, the last of the Neolithic hunters, repossessing what we threw away. Below him, the company of the singing river; above him, hawthorn and alder clinging to the rockface. No electricity, no

cash. While all around him the employing mills of Stockport: cotton, corn, flour, printworks, bleachworks, dyeworks, hatworks – Albert, Victoria, Coronation, Britannia, California, Virginia, India, Spring Bank, Crow Park, Throstle Grove, were washed away, one by one. **PP**

Above: The Blue Pyramid. Looking west along the M60 from the bridge on the A6, Wellington Rd North, near Stockport Town Centre. This is Junction 1, start of the numbering system.

Abney Hall - In 1847 Alfred Orrel, Cotton Merchant, died in one of the few habitable rooms of his half-finished Tudor-style villa in Cheadle. It was called 'The Grove' after his own Grove Printworks (for cloth) which together with its reservoirs had occupied the site.

Two years later the shell was bought by James Watts of Didsbury, wholesale draper. A militant non-conformist, he renamed the place Abney in honour of his namesake, the seventeenth century hymn-writer Isaac Watts whose home was Abney Park near London.

James Watts was one of those men who did spectacularly well out of the rise of Manchester. He built the most spectacular warehouse of them all, now the Britannia Hotel, at the corner of Piccadilly Gardens, and he was able, using the same architects (Travis & Magnall) to turn Abney Hall into a spectacular mansion. He had the interiors decorated in rich Gothic style by J. G. Crace & Son of London, using designs made by A.W.N. Pugin in 1852, right at the end of latter's short life – he died that year, aged only 40.

Watts had visited the Great Exhibition at the Crystal Palace in Hyde Park in 1851 and especially liked the Medieval Court; he wanted everything at Abney to be of the best – Minton tiles, Hardman metalwork, Myers carving. His home became a parvenu's paradise, stuffed with olde English furniture, ancestral heraldry, suits of armour, historical paintings and cheerful mottoes.

Watts was also instrumental as Chairman in arranging in 1857 the first national exhibition of works of art in Britain – the Art Treasures Exhibition – in Manchester rather than London. The newly rich cotton barons of the Northwest had been quietly buying up 'modern' artists for some time, and were persuaded to loan their works – Queen Victoria also lent 39 from the royal collections.

Above: The Manchester Art
Treasures Exhibition 1857:
Queen Victoria and Prince Albe[rt]
together with the future Edwar[d]
VII at the Art Treasures Palace.
The structural debt to the
Crystal Palace is visible.
Goddess to the right.

Above: Abney Hall. The study
1912: It is already heavily
cluttered with sixty years' of
collecting. Most of these items
were dispersed at the great sale
1958.

A special building – the Art Treasures Palace was erected at Old Trafford, in construction similar to the Crystal Palace, built of (then) very futuristic cast iron and glass with a white and red brick frontage. The hanging of the paintings was done against a more traditional lining of wood and painted canvas on the stark cast iron panels. A special station was built at Old Trafford with an 800 foot platform. Charles Hallé (originally a German, Karl Halle, who in 1848 had fled European revolutions to England, this *Land ohne eigene Musik*), was invited to form a 50 piece orchestra to perform daily in the Art Treasures Palace: the Hallé Orchestra survives as Britain's oldest, now lodged in Manchester's Bridgewater Hall. The Exhibition was opened by Prince Albert, and on 29 June Queen Victoria herself attended, and knighted Watts. This must have seemed the pinnacle of his public and commercial life.

His son, also James Watts, continued the embellishment of Abney. In 1893-94 he commissioned George Faulkner Armitage of Altrincham to double the size of the house, in what has been called 'his quaint, exaggerated but mechanical Arts-and-Crafts manner'. Antiquarian, collector and photographer, James Watts II spent many happy weekends pedaling off into the countryside with Fletcher Moss of Didsbury (just up the road) in search of old houses. His photographs can be seen in the seven volumes of Fletcher Moss's *'Pilgrimages to Old Homes'* (see: *Junction 3: Barnes Hospital & Alderman Fletcher Moss.*) There is a suggestion that Watts used the Pilgrimages to scout out old furniture which was then purchased to adorn his great mansion – in fact in the case of Hyde Hall (Junction 25) he bought the whole place.

When James Watts II died in 1926 he was buried under a fine red granite tombstone in front of the Congregational church at Heaton Mersey, which he had supported and beautified all his life. In 1987 the church was demolished. No attempt was made at preservation or salvage. A JCB digger – oops! – broke the stone in half, whereupon the last resting place of one of the richest and most influential men in the history of Manchester was simply cleared and built upon.

When his son, James Watts III, died in 1958, a great sale of the contents was held. The auction took 10 days to sell in 4000 lots what it had taken three lifetimes and a century of collecting to accumulate. The whole house had been valued in 1912 for insurance purposes, and reached the sum of £34,150-5s-0d , perhaps worth £1mn in modern money – could the items still be bought today. A few stray pieces can still be seen at places like Bramall Hall (access via Junction 27 and A5102).

Abney Hall was then used as the Cheadle Town Hall until Cheadle UDC was swallowed up by Stockport in the local Government reorganisation of 1974. It was for a time Byrom's School of Languages. Since then it has been used as offices, with more offices built inside the walled garden. Today the great house is stripped of its splendours, deserted at weekends and in the evenings. But it is just possible, on a summer's night, to imagine the blaze of light from the many leaded windows, the glitter of chandeliers and gold leaf, voices, music, the scent of orchids in the conservatory as, after dinner Sir James Watts, knighted by Queen Victoria at the Art Treasures Palace in 1857 and Lord Mayor of Manchester, conducts the latest group of distinguished visitors – Prince Albert, Gladstone, Disraeli – round his cherished collection. **MH**

Above: Abney Hall in May 1857. Prince Albert departs from Abney Hall where he was the guest of James Watts, Lord Mayor of Manchester, after opening the Art Treasures Exhibition in Old Trafford on 5 May 1857. Watts was knighted when Queen Victoria visited the Exhibition in June that year.

Right: Abney Hall. Drawing Room with fireplace and mirror. Note the fine reflected plaster moulding of the ceiling, and the rich Pugin wallpaper.

Above: Tombstone of James
Watts II. It was destroyed by a
JCB during the demolition of
Heaton Mersey Congregational
Church in 1987

Left: James Watts II.

Agatha Christie at Abney - Abney has one small secret: it was here that Agatha Christie fled to recuperate after her mysterious disappearance and 'loss of memory' in Harrogate in December 1926. Madge, her favourite sister was married to James Watts III, heir to his Lord Mayor grandfather's colonial export business, and by 1926 to Abney Hall also.

But the Watts business acumen was declining: in the 1870s the Hall had passed to the second James Watts, whose fortune allowed him time and leisure to be an amateur photographer and antiquarian. By the third generation, a Watts son was a theatre owner in Manchester, another an actor. Nonetheless, life at Abney seems to have continued as late a Victorian idyll. As a young girl, Agatha Christie and her widowed mother regularly from 1903 lived part of their winters here and at nearby Cheadle Hall, looking after Jack, the son of James and Madge, while his parents went off to St Moritz for the skating. At Christmas Abney filled up with the six Watts children for a period of theatre visits to Manchester, jigsaws in the jigsaw room, charades –

with the young Agatha appearing at dinner as a 'Turkish Lady' who belched her way approvingly through the meal. There were inordinate amounts of food which the Christies, *mère et fille*, living in straitened circumstance, could ill afford at home in Ealing.

Abney was Agatha Christie's comfort zone, and it was to here that she fled when her married life became unbearable. Whatever the truth of her amnesia in 1926, the opulence of Abney and the Watts had early slid into Agatha Christie's unconscious, to reappear in the foreword to *Adventures of the Christmas Pudding* (published 1960 and dedicated to Abney Hall): "The Christmas fare"

she wrote in fond and girlish style of those remembered crisp Edwardian winters "was of gargantuan proportions."

Abney Hall occurs in even grander form as 'Chimneys' in *The Secret of Chimneys* (published 1925, dedicated to nephew Jack Watts) and as 'Gorston Hall' in *Hercule Poirot's Christmas* (published 1938, dedicated to Jimmy Watts, her brother-in-law). Two of the characters in *'They Do It With Mirrors'* (1952) drown in the 'Fish Pond' at Abney – dark, overgrown and still a little ominous today. So, Abney Hall has, in addition to

Prince Albert, Gladstone and Disraeli, also entertained both Hercule Poirot and Miss Marple. There is of course (or at least used to be) a secret tunnel under the drive...

Nearby is Chorlton Brook, which passes through the sad wild grounds of the Park, under a vandalized rockery bridge, and drops away around the Fish Pond, to run beneath the M60 in a culvert. It falls at last into the Micker Brook and both then lose themselves in the Mersey. Potent stuff, literature. Sad place, Abney. **PP**

Above: Abney Hall Fish Pond. Looking across the fish pond towards Abney Hall. Just 10 yards or so behind is the M60 motorway and M56 interchange at Junction 4. The Fish Pond is the scene of several murders in Agatha Christie novels.

Right: Steps at Abney Hall.
West facade of Abney Hall,
comprising the original house
and the 1911 extension with
round bay windows.

Barnes Hospital - This great gaunt pile of a building, abandoned and all dark at night, except for the lonely light in its tower-top clock, is not just near Junction 3 but embraced by it. If you come off the M60 Eastbound onto the A34 you gyrate right around it.

So that's the M60 Orbital Motorway and a major north-south artery to contend with. Add three railway lines, several lesser roads and two rivers and it is clear that this is an extraordinary concatenation of man-made and natural geography.

The Barnes Convalescent Home at Cheadle, 'a valuable auxiliary to the noble work of the Manchester Royal Infirmary' (formerly in central Manchester at Piccadilly) was built in the 1870s to provide recuperating patients with fresh air, perfect quietness, and skilled attention. Three times a week an omnibus left the MRI carrying patients out to Cheadle.

The foundation stone was laid on July 29th 1871 and Barnes Hospital was opened in October 1875. Described at the time as a handsome and spacious building in the gothic style, it was designed by

Messrs. Blackwell & Booth, architects of Bury. The builders were Thomas Clay & Son of Audenshaw. The exterior was said to be devoid of elaborate superfluous decoration, but we might perhaps disagree with this today, after eyeing up the wearisome notchiness and polychromy of its monstrous exterior. The total cost was something like £52,000 (say £4 mn today), of which half came from Mr Robert Barnes.

The Barneses lived in some style at Oakley, a brick Tudor villa in Fallowfield, which is now the USDAW Headquarters (Union of Shop, Distributive and Allied Workers), and hence it is preserved. Robert Barnes was Lord Mayor of Manchester in the 1850s. The Barnes Convalescent Home at Cheadle was one of several good works carried out by Robert Barnes in memory of his only son, also Robert, who died in

eft: Agatha Christie at Abney
Hall. Perhaps as Prince Charming
in an amateur theatrical.
She appears to be standing in
front of the waterfall in the
grounds. Undated photograph,
possibly 1912.

POLICE DOGS
IN TRAINING
ENTER AT YOUR
OWN RISK

Left: Barnes Hospital. Since it was vacated, Barnes Hospital has been used by Greater Manchester Police as a place to train its dogs. A residential development is in planning.

1866. Barnes was a Wesleyan, but his son had been training for the Anglican church when he died suddenly in Oxford. There was also the Barnes Home For Destitute Boys at Heaton Mersey, another hideous but well-meaning pile, now alas gone, as well as a Barnes Samaritan Charity, and the gift of a lifeboat at Abersoch in Wales, named 'Mabel Louisa' after his daughter.

Robert Barnes senior and his brother Thomas were partners in a cotton business at Jackson Street in Manchester. Both retired with handsome fortunes. Robert purchased an estate in Herefordshire called Harefield, but got bored and came back to Manchester. He died in 1870. Mabel Louisa, namesake of the lifeboat, inherited her father's benevolence as well as his money. She was executor of her father's will, mostly left to charity. She paid

for a new chancel at St James' Church Didsbury in 1871 (architects Horton and Bridgford), and two stained glass windows at the west end. Her own memorial is in the south wall of the church near the Mosley monument.

At the Barnes Hospital order and regularity were the rule. At 6.30 a.m. nurses and servants assembled in the chapel, naturally, then went about their duties until 8 a.m. when the more able patients went to the dining hall for breakfast. The Medical Officer did his rounds in the morning till a good northern 'Dinner' at 12 noon. Tea followed at 5 p.m., Supper at 8:00. Then bed. There were usually 130 patients at a time; 1,600 or so over a year. Newer building, including a gym and a morgue, were added latterly, in 1970s utilitarian non-style with flat roofs. Perhaps 1870s bombast is preferable after all. Just enough of the

Above: Barnes Hospital is now boarded up, it has housed sick Mancunians, recovering war veterans and asylum seekers

gardens survive, (originally extending to 46 acres), to give the building a setting and a buffer from the ceaseless M60 and M56 Motorway traffic.

The hospital carried on its original function until about 1993, including treating wounded soldiers in the First War, and was also used briefly to house 'asylum seekers.' Since then it has stood empty and boarded up on its motorway island.

When Barnes hospital was being built in the 1870s an Anglo-Saxon preaching cross was uncovered in the grounds – intriguing because there is no mention of a church here at Domesday in 1086. At Cheadle we are at the edge of the Mercian Saxon advance to the Mersey just across the M60, and the very name Cheadle shows a confusing mix of Welsh speaking residents ('coed' – a wood) and Saxons – 'lea' a clearing. Beyond here were the Northumbrians with their own dialect, or pagan Danes and Vikings. Border country, and probably dangerous for soldier and missionary alike. **MH**

Alderman Fletcher Moss - Fletcher Moss is not a place, although it sounds like one. Fletcher Moss is, or was, a person. He lived at the Old Parsonage at Didsbury, opposite St James' parish church, though he was emphatically not a parson. Born in 1845, he lived there from about 1864 and died there in 1919. He was of a type – dare we suggest it? – still prevalent in Didsbury.

Independent, outspoken, finicky about his diet, cantankerous. Fletcher Moss was also a bicyclist – probably owning a velocipede. In 1900 bicycles were distinctly racy; a cyclist was a modern man, a free spirit. He used to load his bicycle onto the train at Didsbury station (long since closed – oh, those happy days! And not yet re-opened as part of the Metrolink) and take it to, well, all over the place. Much Wenlock, Clun, Tintern, Montgomery. Nor did he travel alone – James Watts of Abney Hall (see *Junction 2: Abney Hall*) was his constant companion. When they returned home, always on the same day, Fletcher Moss would write an account of his adventures in trenchant prose, and James Watts, would retire to his darkroom to develop the glass plates exposed during the trip. The resulting 'Pilgrimages', first published in 1901, eventually filled six volumes, plus a seventh, slimmer one, published after Moss' death. It is evident from the short obituary that opens this last volume that Watts, self-effacing as always, had underwritten the cost of publishing them all.

Fletcher Moss was also an alderman, serving on the council of the burgeoning city of Manchester faithfully if, no doubt, argumentatively. He was the prime mover in the provision of a library for Didsbury, going down to London in 1913 to meet

Andrew Carnegie to solicit the cash, not only for Didsbury but for Withington and Chorlton as well.

When Fletcher Moss died in 1919 he gave his house, everything in it, and his beautiful garden, to the people of the city he loved, to be cared for by the council he had served for so many years. Whereupon the City immediately sold all the contents. Both the house and the garden are commonly called Fletcher Moss today, and it is possible that one day the whole area, once the old village of Didsbury (before the centre moved half a mile up the road to be near the railway), will be called Fletcher Moss. And why not – fashionable East Didsbury has already split from more staid West Didsbury, while the property developers are rapidly throwing up Didsbury Point, with the Manchester Municipal Necropolis of the Southern Cemetery on one side, and on the other what remains of Chorlton Union Workhouse. A sort of social Alzheimer's for place names. **MH**

Above: The Parsonage, Fletcher Moss, Didsbury. Ornate stone gateway to Didsbury parsonage and garden, under snow, 7th Dec 2002. Through the gateway is Wilmslow Road and the Didsbury Campus of Manchester Metropolitan University.

Left: Fletcher Moss on Horseback. Taken in front of the Old Parsonage, Didsbury.

The Salmon Ladder At Northenden - Passers and Drinkers-Up at the Tatton Arms on Boat Lane may have been puzzled in 2003 by the works taking place in the bed of the river Mersey in front of the pub. There has always been a weir here, built to create a head of water for the old Northenden Mill. It is, believe it or not, a salmon ladder, more like a salmon slalom actually, designed to allow migrating salmon to by-pass the weir. Salmon, in Manchester? Yes! In pre-industrial times the Mersey was a famous salmon river. Now they are returning.

If you are feeling suicidal about the state of the world, remember the quiet environmental triumph of the Cleansing of the Mersey. All this in view of the M60, sweeping grandly by on an elevated section over the Mersey and Palatine Road.

There are old traditions that salmon and trout were caught as high as the centre of Manchester on the Irwell in the 1820s, and indeed as high as Prestwich in 1825. At New Bailey Bridge near the Law Courts in Central Manchester other smaller fish were described as being in shoals, and innumerable. One 18lb salmon even got as far as Warrington as late as 1840, though half dead from pollution, particularly from the gasworks, sewage and offal.

Above: The Salmon Ladder on
the Mersey at Northenden

Left: Palatine Road at Northenden. Looking from Palatine Road bridge over the River Mersey towards St Wilfrid's Church at Northenden and the Tatton Arms pub on the left. Above is the motorway viaduct; nearby is Junction 5.

Northenden Weir was a famous spot for jollification. 'The banks of the river became a busy bustling Bacchanalium, where boating men and beanfeasters made boisterous revels at weekends and holidays'. So Fletcher Moss recalled in typically alliterative prose. The ancient pub was rebuilt in 1874 for the Tattons of Wythenshawe Hall by the architect James Redford in a determinedly jolly style, all fancy brickwork, timber framing and fretted bargeboards. It is a pity that an extension on the left-hand end has made it elephantine.

The white-painted building at the back, with more tricky brickwork, was the pub stable. Now it is the Northenden theatre club. MH

Above: Northenden from the Mersey Idealised mid-Victorian view of Northenden looking from Lancashire into Cheshire, with embanked Mersey, St Wilfrid's Church and skiff ferry. The footbridge was not built until the 1870s.

Rose Hill: *Total Amnesia* - Sir Edward Watkin (1819-1901) was another of those Victorians who made Manchester great. Not just Manchester either, but England and, if he had got his way, Europe and the world too. He was the Railway King.

A visionary promoter and suave committee man, he supported engineering projects and railways across the world. He was President of the Grand Trunk Railway of Canada, which was the unifying link that effectively created and held together that country. If Sir Ed had got his way, we would have got a channel tunnel a century earlier than we eventually did, and we would have a Scotland-Ireland tunnel too. We would have had an Eiffel tower in Wembley. As it is, he was the promoter of many railway schemes with grand intentions, the Great Central, the Trent Valley (or Birmingham main-line by-pass). More locally, he ran the Cheshire Lines. He was a man of politics and letters too, a Liberal M.P. and biographer of Cobden, corn law reformer.

Watkin lived at Northenden. Rose Hill had been bought by his father, Absolom Watkin, in the 1830s, and turned into a little paradise. With its southern aspect, its beechwoods, its prospect over the wide Mersey valley, its closeness to the pretty Cheshire village of Northenden with its old church and ferry, it had everything going for it. Its gardens were famous. Sir Edward improved Rose Hill, adding wide porches and bay windows and expanding the library.

Time has not been kind to Rose Hill. Almost everything that blessed it has been taken away, even its name, and indeed the house itself has only survived by the skin of its teeth. The village of Northenden is now in Manchester, part of Wythenshawe. The old church was mostly rebuilt in the 1870s. Rose Hill's garden and parkland is under houses. Even the view has gone – for where is the Mersey? It was moved, diverted, with the building of the M60, so now a glittering two-way river of mobile machinery fills the valley where the placid stream used to be.

As for the old house, when Watkin died it was sold, and followed a fairly predictable fate – convalescent home, hospital, orphanage and finally remand home. In the 1979 Manchester received a fantastic windfall: an enormous painting, left at Rose Hill because it was too big to go anywhere else, was identified as The Icebergs, by the American painter Frederick Edwin Church, and raised £2mn at Sotheby's. It didn't save the old house though, which, when the remand home closed, was left to decay to a mere shell. It is now being done up as flats called, insultingly, Ashley Grange. Why? The only instantly recognisable feature is the huge erratic boulder (12 tons) that still stand on a stalk at the side of the house. Like the picture, too big to move.

Of Sir Edward's great schemes, many came to nought, or – more interestingly – were only realised long after his death. We now have the channel tunnel, the giant ferris wheel. His continental gauge main line, the Great Central, may yet be revived. Meanwhile the old Cheshire Lines chunter on, transporting thousands in greater or lesser delight through Oxford Road station. And, just outside the gates of Rose Hill, a tall signal box keeps guard over Northenden Junction, on the Cheshire Lines. **MH**

Above: 'Rose Hill' Hidden between Sharston Industrial Estate, Didsbury Golf Course, Loonts Lake and Junctions 4 and 5 of the M60, it is pictured here in February 1998. It has since been restored as part of a housing development.

The Mummy on the Priory Roof - There are certain people who seem to be sent from the past to warn us: Hannah Beswick, a.k.a. the 'Grey Lady of Birchen Bower', is one such. She represents that restlessness which propels people around motorways like the M60 – except that she travelled her route between 1758 and 1868, mostly while dead and mummified, occasionally as a ghost.

Dr White, her embalmer and keeper, has bequeathed his name to the Sale area. He died in 1813 but his family name survives in White's Bridge, at Dane Road, over the Bridgewater Canal. Hannah Beswick has vanished without trace, and her story has been distorted beyond recognition.

She lived in a large manor house (now demolished) called Birchen Bower at Hollinwood near Oldham, now right next to Junction 22. She died in 1758, but not before witnessing the arrival of Bonny Prince Charlie in Manchester in 1745 – Manchester then being radical Jacobite. She had two severe shocks

about this time: she buried her money, but failed to dig it up; and her beloved brother John was nearly interred alive. He had actually been placed in his coffin and it was only just before the lid was to be screwed down that it was noticed that his eyelids were flickering. A check by the Doctor, Charles White, showed that he was still alive. He was taken from his coffin and woke from his coma a few days later, to live on for many more years.

This event created such an impression on Hannah Beswick that she immediately made out her will, leaving the whole of her estate to Doctor White: he was to receive the income from the Birchen Bower as long as Hannah's body was not buried, but embalmed and kept above ground. Every twenty one years the body was to be taken back to Birchen House and left in the Granary for twenty four hours. Shortly before her death, Hannah told her relatives that she would show them the location of her hidden gold. However, her condition deteriorated and she died a few days later, taking her secret with her.

Doctor White had her body embalmed in tar and swathed it in heavy bandages, leaving the face uncovered. The corpse was then placed in a glass-fronted coffin and was kept at Doctor White's in Manchester before being moved, on his retirement, to the roof of his house called Sale Priory. On his death in 1813 it went to the Museum of the Manchester Natural History Society in Peter Street, Manchester.

Hannah Beswick was on public display in Peter Street in what in fact looked suspiciously like a grandfather clock case, from about 1828 until 1868 when the Society became the present Manchester Museum. De Quincey (of opium eater fame) then a Manchester Grammar School boy (motto: Dare to be Wise), and already displaying morbid interest in these matters, tried to impress a lady friend by trying, but failing, to gain an audience with the Mummy.

On the creation of the modern Manchester Museum, Hannah's relatives did not wish to be responsible for the disposal of her remains. This seems unkind – the relatives had been allowed the privilege of free entry to visit her if they wished, during the time of her residence with the Society. With the permission of the Bishop of Manchester, Hannah Beswick was buried in Harpurhey Cemetery in an unmarked grave on 22nd July 1868. It was said to be a condition of Hannah Beswick's will that her body should be taken back to Birchen Bower every 21 years. According to tradition, the

body was laid to rest for the specified period in the old barn. But strange things happened on the estate. Horses and cattle, secured in their stables and paddocks overnight, were found loose in the fields the following morning. On one occasion a cow was found up in the hayloft.

Hannah began to appear in the old house, by then subdivided. A rustling of silk was followed by the apparition of a lady in black, who would glide through the room towards the parlour, where she would disappear at one particular flagstone. A poor weaver finally struck it lucky: he discovered Hannah's hidden hoard of 'gold wedges' under the floor, whilst digging a treadle-hole to fit a new loom in the parlour, at the very spot where Hannah Beswick was seen so many times to disappear. He sold the wedges to a gold dealer called Oliphants in St Ann's Square Manchester, for £3/10s/- each, at a time when a labourer was lucky to earn £1 in a week.

Hannah Beswick is still said to haunt the area of the site on which Birchen Bower once stood. In April, 1956, several night-shift workers claimed to have seen her shadowy figure at the Ferranti Works. She was also seen standing at the works' entrance in 1968. In 1972, she was seen wandering through the works' canteen. There was another reported sighting in 1981.

Sadly, not much of the above appears to be true. Hannah's will is extant, and does not mention embalming or exposure of her corpse at Birchen Bower. Her heirs and relatives argued over the terms, and Birchen Bower was still being disputed in the 1860s. Doubtless a malevolent ghost and buried treasure were convenient propaganda weapons in their battle. Dr Charles White (1728-1813) was a respected Manchester surgeon, who helped set up the first maternity hospital in Manchester; his views on hygiene were far in advance of his

Above: Hannah Beswick, The Manchester Mummy: here depicted, in transit, on the roof of Dr White's house at Sale Priory.

time, and he was successful in reducing both infant mortality and puerperal fever. In 1773 he wrote the classic guide: "The Management of Pregnant and Lying-in Women."

Meanwhile Hannah Beswick's visits to Birchen Bower have grown erratic and out of character – she was last sighted wearing a sartorial anachronism – a Trilby hat. **PP**

Sale Water Park - (originally *The Sale Ees Water Sports Park Concept*) is a curiously successful solution to the problem of embanking the M60 to a height of up to 34 feet along the Mersey floodplain. The success of the Water Park is not evident from the 1972 Department of the Environment brochure on this 4 mile stretch of the motorway.

This publication manages, without blush, to avoid any mention of the Environment, plants or wildlife, or indeed of any environmental impact. The main obsession is with concrete – nearly 50,000 cubic metres of it, and 5,000 tonnes of steel. Attitudes have indeed changed in the intervening 30 years.

Importing the large amounts of soil need for the embanking operation was prohibitive in terms of cost and disruption. So it was decided to excavate the material from a vast hole – thirty five football pitches wide, which would later double up as flood control storage capacity, and a sports facility. Sale Water Park was born: and local folklore has it that a yellow motorway dumper truck still lies submerged deep in its waters.

More seriously, the M60 here does not drain into the existing watercourses – this would in time of flood allow the River Mersey to rise up monstrously through the M60's sewers, and reclaim the motorway. So the M60 has its own run-off channels.

Withington Golf Course became part of this entire flood control system, with culverts under the motorway allowing floodwaters to pass to the south. Furthermore, the River Mersey, its signature till then a loopy orthography, saw its meanders curtailed at both ends so that the Motorway would not need to cross it at multiple points. As well, however, to remember that a River is only tamed for a while: you cannot build permanent structures over a strong brown god. **PP**

Right: Sale Water Park New Bridge (2004). One of several new footbridges, seen here on 8 July 2004, erected as part of the widening scheme for Junctions 5-8. This one links Sale Water Park with Sale near the site of Sale Priory.

Above: Sunset at Sale Water
Park. Sunset at Sale Water
Park, 26 July 2003. The lake
was formed by excavation of
soil and gravel to build the
M60 embankment.

Fengshui, Leylines & Cheeses - If there is any truth in Chinese 'fengshui' or Alfred Watkins' Leylines, then this is the place in Manchester where these all gather into one knot and bundle. A place where the lines of power, the dragon's spine, are literally made manifest. Perhaps it is the navel of Manchester.

Perhaps it is the navel of Manchester. Because here is the Great Intersection, the conjunction at the Mersey of the M60 motorway (AD 1957-1998) with the A56 trunk road (Roman), the Bridgewater Canal (AD 1760), the Metrolink and the railway to Chester (AD 1849), the Manchester section of the National Cycleway (passing under the M60 next to the Railway), and the Transpennine Trail (passing under the M60 by a culvert as a footpath). The electricity pylons also cut through here. There is even a set of stepping stones over brooding Sale Water. Previously there was also a ferry here - Jackson's Boat across the Mersey. The Barrow, Ousel and Chorlton Brooks are also nearby. This is also a place where disused arms of the Mersey languish – inexplicable dry grooves in the landscape.

In contrast to the predictable numbered bridges of the M60, there are several named bridges here – Eye Platt Bridge, Eye Platt New Bridge (both on the A56). These 'eyes' are small islands – we are in the Mersey floodplain. Barfoot Bridge carries both the Bridgewater Canal and the Metrolink, while Cut Hole Bridge stands a little to the North in Stretford. White's Bridge (after Beswick's embalmer) and Crossford Bridge lie to the south in Sale. The name Stretford gives the game away: this where the Romans chose to locate their access to Mamucium, where the Roman street forded the Mersey.

And the Mersey, ancient boundary between Northumbria and Mercia, Lancashire and Cheshire,

has not moved as much as you might suspect. Its line in 1636, at Northenden at least, was the same as today, already embanked against its surges from rainfall in the distant Peaks.

The boundary between Stretford and Chorlton still runs down the middle of the Mersey here – curious to impose a line on a map onto a constantly flowing and changing body of uncontrollable water. But this was always flood plain – Chorlton Ees, Eye Platt, the Washway (A56). The appropriately named Highfield Road is the first road you meet in Stretford as the land rises. On the south side at Sale it is Booth Road – perhaps where cowmen had their summer booths while they pastured their cattle on the water meadows below and thought of cheese. You might be forgiven for thinking it was Cheshire cheese, but it was in fact Lancashire: the River moved north over the centuries, stranding a little bit of Lancashire to the south.

Cheshire or Lancashire cheese ? The two cheeses are very similar, generally white and crumbly. Traditionally Cheshire cheeses, which are round, and may be red, white or blue, were made with milk from cows that had been pastured on meadows around the salt mines, or on the estuary salt flats, giving its

distinctive salty tang. These cheeses were made in every farm cellar on stone slabs, with a well of cold water nearby. They were sometimes a condition of leases – still paid for example to the Stanleys of Alderley in the early nineteenth century. The British Navy dropped Suffolk cheese in the 1750s –'a thin, hard and durable variety, but practically inedible' in favour of full cream Cheshire, which was both dry and salty, and so had good keeping qualities. 10,000 tons are said to have been sent to London every year, doubtless also to the famous Cheshire Cheese Inn at the Law Courts. A grinning Cheshire Cat is said to have been stamped onto the surface.

Lancashire cheese also had a reputation – 'Leigh Toaster' being best for toasted welsh rarebit. The Second War effectively destroyed the tradition – 202 farms made it in 1939, but only 22 by 1948. It was best produced by mixing in the previous day's curds. Today the unpasteurised process is limited to only three Lancashire farms.

The whole Junction 7 area has been extensively excavated three times in the past three centuries – in the 1750s for the Bridgewater Canal embankment, in the 1840s for the Manchester railway line

Above: M60 Junction 7 (forme M63) Boundary Viaduct carryir the Motorway over the Cheste Manchester railway line and the Bridgewater Canal. The Metrolink and the Transpennir Cycle Route also pass under th M60 Motorway here. Artist's impression, 1972 for the Sale Eastern and Nothenden By-Pas M63, now M60.

embankment, and in the 1970s when the M63 (now M60) was built, and the large hole at Sale Water Park excavated for gravel. The canal allowed the growth of market gardens in Sale, providing vegetables and flowers to Manchester.

James Brindley had to get the canal of his patron the Duke of Bridgewater across this marshy declivity. He had already thrown the canal over the Irwell on an aqueduct at Barton. His solution here was another aqueduct: Barfoot bridge over the River Mersey, followed by a 17 foot (c. 5.5 meter) embankment over the boggy ground. It is odd to think of a canal being inundated and drowned, rather than bursting its banks, but global warming will doubtless bring many revolutions in our thought patterns.

One of Brindley's canal models, as demonstrated to a Parliamentary Select Committee, was reportedly made of cheese (origin unspecified) – plainly an original thinker. Yet this was big business: in the 1790s the first American cotton to Manchester came by this canal via Merseyside. And by 1800 the mills of Manchester were running mainly on steam, fired up by nearly 50,000 tons of coal a year, much of it carried by canal barges from the Duke's collieries at the Worsley end. (see Junction 13: *Worsley – Underground Delves*). Some of these barges were also steam driven as early as 1799. By 1816 Manchester was making enough yarn in one year (313 million miles) to tie the moon to Manchester over a thousand times. Probably not today.

This Sale flood plain is still given over to temporary and seasonal occupations, where flooding can be accepted by the occupiers – Sale Water Park (where the lake has itself swallowed up the Chorlton-cum-Hardy Victorian sewage works and its persistent odour), Crossford Bridge Sports Centre and Recreation Ground, cricket grounds, playing fields, golf courses – and cemeteries, where complaints from residents about flooding are few. In the eighteenth and

nineteenth century the area saw ice skating when it flooded and froze in winter – global warming has now put paid to freezing winters as far North as Alaska; but flooding may be back on the cards. Perhaps the M60 and its motor cars, generating emissions to the last, will be swept aside in one last inundation in the tradition of the great Manchester floods of 1828, 1840, 1841 and 1881. **PP**

St Martin and his Geese at Ashton-On-Mersey - The Carrington Spur (A6144(M)) is a motorway oddity because it is a single-carriageway two-way road subject to motorway rules. It crosses the river Mersey where there must have been an ancient crossing from Ashton-on-Mersey Church.

Left: Crossford Bridge, Toll Bar and Toll House in 1882. The bay-window on the Toll House allowed the keeper to see approaching traffic – still mainly horse drawn. The toll charge was abolished in 1885. This is now the A56, passing over the Mersey to Junction 7.

The church tower can be seen above the trees. Reaching it involves some tricky navigation along narrow and surprisingly countrified lanes. The church itself is at the end of the road – beyond it is only the flat floodplain of the Mersey. It is a very curious little building, but before looking at the building itself it is important to weigh up the topography. From every angle of approach the church stands up, on a mound. Only a few feet high to be sure, but significant.

A lane leads beyond the church towards the river, to an ancient crossing-point into Lancashire. Another goes along the side of the churchyard, parallel with the river. Now imagine the great marshy vale of the mazy Mersey as it was before the river was tamed. A crossroads of two hazardous but important packhorse routes. And where the roads cross, a dry island, only a few feet high but commanding the whole valley. It was important: a notable stopping point and meeting place.

The church itself is comical little building made up of disparate parts. The bits that hit you first are the Victorian additions. The big Lychgate and the extraordinary Belltower, both very bold and eccentric, were built in 1887 by the Rev Joseph Ray, vicar, and Sir William Cunliffe Brooks, banker, who lived at Barlow Hall across the river. George Trufitt (1824-1902) was the architect. Trufitt also designed

the small but richly sculptural Lombardy Chambers in Manchester town, which was Brooks's Bank.

The little church, in beautifully weathered warm stone, is a low building dated 1714 on the porch, with very large Gothick windows at the ends. Sir Joshua Allen built it out of nearby Lymm stone. But there must have been an earlier church, for the parish dates from 1304. This first church, probably timber-framed like Warburton old church a few miles downriver, was built by John de Carrington and William de Sala (perhaps Sale). The great storm of 1704 wrecked it. That is as far back as we can go with confidence. Who knows what stood here before then. A Roman Camp? A Saxon burial place?

The church is dedicated to St Martin of Tours in France. Rather oddly, he was associated with the migration of geese, which surely would have been a big feature along the Mersey valley. He might have been intrigued by the recent invasion of Canada Geese, which have taken over from native varieties (see *Birds on the M60*)

Above: The church and graveyard of St Martin at Ashton-upon-Mersey. The Church is built on a slightly raised bank in this low-lying area.

The Trafford Centre: *The Orbital Emporium* - Let us begin with the facts. The concept was born in 1984, that is, some years before the orbital M60 was complete. In 1986 the planning application was submitted. It was a long haul, going as far as the House of Lords, but finally in 1995 planning permission was granted.

In May 1996 construction started, and on September 10th 1998 the Trafford Retail Centre opened for business. The architects were Chapman Taylor & Partners of London, the site architects Leach, Rhodes, Walker of Manchester and the construction engineers Bovis. It was a greenfield site, the land having remained agricultural until the 1980s. The Trafford Centre, The Manchester Ship Canal, Chat Moss, and the John Lennon Airport Liverpool, are all owned by Peel Holdings plc. Statistically the Trafford Centre can be summarised as the first, the biggest, and the mostest. Here are some quotations which reveal to us the 'vision thing'

'Location - served by two junctions on Manchester's orbital

Motorway, scheduled for completion around the time of opening, the Trafford Centre will be READILY ACCESSIBLE to motorists from the entire region and beyond.'

'A powerful shopping machine'

'Inward-looking, but glazed malls of extrovert character. Half of all visitors enter at ground level and half at first floor level. The glazed domes over the central malls define the Centre when viewed from a distance. From the spacious, airy shopping malls to car parking, the Trafford Centre will provide a safe, secure and comfortable environment.'

An Architectural Critique

Not many people go to the Trafford Centre to look at

the architecture. Nevertheless the architecture is a vital part of the package, creating the image and ambience to attract shoppers from near and far and to encourage them to spend freely when they get there. How is it done? The architects and designers had a clean slate to work on. The Trafford Centre could have looked like anything or nothing. It could have been purely utilitarian, with its steel and concrete structure on view and all its pipes showing.

It could have been covered all over in yellow lavatory tiles, like the Arndale Centre in the middle of Manchester, which a 3000lb (1.7 tonne) IRA bomb miserably failed to destroy in June 1996. Where do you start? A quotation from another vision of the past may help:

'The space itself offers no circumstances …. to fetter or lead the designer's mind. It is an opportunity for an almost purely

Above: Trafford Centre Sunset. Sunset over the Trafford Centre with the dome and one of the towers rising into the sky. Red neon lights attempt to recreate the effect of fire.

bove: The Orient, Trafford

entre. a vast hall done up in

e style of an ocean liner, with

ilings, wooden decks and

eboats. A big screen is built

to the superstructure of the

hip', with an ornamental pool

 the centre. On the ceiling is a

ainted sky with lights for stars.

imaginative composition, so we have columns, piers, cornices, panels, niches, projections and recesses, architraves, pediments, and decorative details, all used as so much material for the artist.'

The quotation above refers not to the Trafford Centre, but to Michelangelo's famous Library at San Lorenzo, Florence for Duke Cosimo di Medici of 1524-34, and especially to the great staircase hall that precedes it.

Faced with a large empty space Michelangelo decked it out with fantastic fake architecture: columns, piers, architraves and all the rest, drawing on his unrivalled knowledge and imagination to create a masterpiece. Here at the Trafford, on a gigantic scale, the designers have done exactly the same thing. It is as though they have raided the pages of Banister Fletcher's *History of Architecture*, and chosen something from every showy style: Egyptian, Roman, Pompeian, Rococo, Baroque.

The outside has to look good at speed from the motorway, or very briefly when searching out a parking spot. The model is an ecclesiastical one, St Peter's in Rome, with its dome and its gesticulating figures along the facade. It even suffers from the same fault as that august prototype (by Michelangelo again) in that the dome, which looks so good from a distance, disappears when close at hand. The Mormons, when they built their Temple to the north on the M61 at Chorley, chose instead a Gothic spire with a golden trumpeter angel on the pinnacle as their landmark, (and run the risk of being mistaken for another swanky retail outlet).

As for the Trafford Centre, it is the inside that counts. That gasp of impressed astonishment which always greets the first view of the sunlit mall curving into the distance with its palm trees (artificial, but with real leaves), the kaleidoscope of polished marble and stones (real, mostly) and the hubbub of happy shoppers is what Peel Holdings plc paid Chapman Taylor & Partners for.

The Trafford Centre is built on two levels, like so many shopping precincts around the world. The model for them all is the medieval Rows at Chester. The problem with every two-level precinct is that the upper level tends to die. Hence the significance of feeding in the punters, willy, nilly, by obligatory car parking at both levels. Chester in 2003, having pedestrianised the streets, could learn something back from the Trafford Centre.

The Trafford Centre could not exist without the M60. Nobody could get there. The promised Metrolink has not materialised. Thus it is automatically selective in its clientele. No loose-cannon kids at school-out time, no Big Issue sellers. And so it can never be an alternative city centre however much it may imitate features of the city centre. Who would have thought of demonstrating against impending war at the Trafford Centre? Nor

would any such intrusion of reality be tolerated for an instant.

What would the de Traffords think of it all ?, This ancient Lancastrian family gave their name to both Old Traffords, to the Trafford Borough, to the Trafford Centre and to the Industrial Park - which was, amazingly, their ancestral demesne. To judge by the way they have always moved with the times, true to their motto 'NOW THUS' they would approve. Patently, it is just what we all want. **MH**

The Trafford Centre: *More Quirky Facts* - The Trafford Centre opened for business on September 10th 1998, after a planning process prolonged by concerns of congestion on the M60 (then M63). It took Bovis 27 months to build, at a cost of £600 mn. It covers 150 acres of what was Dumplington, which still appears on the roadsigns.

The shopping area is equivalent to 26 football pitches. The architectural styles include Classical Roman and Greek, Aztec, Egyptian, Chinese, Ocean Liner and New Orleans. The advertising pylons are known as Totem Poles. The Centre is clad mainly with Italian granites and marbles. Other Trafford stones includes Gabbros, Sandstones, Limestones, and Gneiss. There is no Welsh Slate.

With an annual footfall of approaching 30 million visitors (the same as Manchester Airport), everyone in Britain has by now visited it three times. Some 5.3 mn people (10% of the UK population) live within 45 minutes' drive. Their total potential retail spend is estimated at £13bn. The Trafford Centre is closed on Christmas Day. On Easter Sundays the Centre is open but the shops closed.

About two thirds of all visitors are Mancunian females in employment, so-called 'Stylish Singles' and 'Early Adopters' who live within five miles of the Centre, are from social classes ABC1 (professional, non-manual or skilled), 16 to 44 years old, and come at least once a month for a 'dwell time' of 2 hours and 43 minutes and 'average spend' of precisely £97.02p. Somewhat surprisingly for this key group, 'The Trafford Centre maintains a non-smoking policy throughout the Centre.' Mainly absent from the Centre are 'Independent Elders' 'Low Rise Council' and 'Victorian Low Status.'

Above: Barton Bridge.
Looking from Macro Car Park
to the north of the Manchester
Ship Canal. In the distance are
Trafford Park factories and one
of the blocks of flats in
Pendleton, Salford.

Above: Griffins and Ladies,
Trafford Centre, statues of ladies
playing on pipes and dancing
griffins, holding the letters TC,
('Trafford Centre'). Underneath,
painted in gold, is '1998' - the
year the Trafford Centre opened.

There are 40 restaurants and cafés with 6000 covers. Cuisines include British fish and chips, Italian pizza, Chinese dimsum, as well as East Asian, French, Indian, Spanish, three US varieties (Kentucky Fried Chicken, Tex-Mex and Deep South), and Mediterranean. Braille menus are generally available. The theme countries of The Orient restaurant area are China, Egypt, Italy, the US (with New Orleans) and Morocco. There are 23 separate licences for alcohol. The crèche is sponsored by Milkybar, the Play Area by Smarties – both Nestlé products. In 2004 Manchester's inhabitants were ranked first in the 'fat scores' of UK cities.

There are over 280 shopping outlets, 'five nationally renowned anchor stores,' and twelve cashpoints. The Selfridges' branch was their first outside London and, at nearly 20,000 sq. m. occupies one fifth of total available space at the Centre. About 7,000 people work at the Trafford Centre. The Festival Village area of small independent retailers is being refurbished to accommodate a new John Lewis store, opening 2005.

There are 1.2 million cars within 45 minutes drive of the Centre. There are over 10,000 parking spaces at the Centre, with 65 dedicated disabled spaces. According to the Centre's own publicity, 'Some 25% of visitors travel to the Centre by non-car modes.' The Centre also has a dodgem car facility. The Trafford Centre has its own Trafford Centre Credit Card – the first shopping centre in the UK to issue its own worldwide card. Goods can be ordered via the Centre's website, and are delivered by the Centre. Accounts can also be managed online, thus avoiding all need to visit the Centre.

The Trafford Centre provides teachers with Curriculum Resource Packs for Key Stages 3 and 4, suitable for geography, maths, ICT, English, Drama and, of course, Business Studies. These are £25.00 each, plus VAT and postage.

There are twenty cinema screens seating 28,500 customers a week – the busiest in the UK. The UCI cinemas can also be hired for large business meetings. The cinemas close at 03:00 a.m. on Sunday morning. There is also an 18 lane ten-pin bowling alley.

There are 101 security officers, 350 CCTV cameras and six plain-clothes security personnel. The main offences targetted are shoplifting, theft from cars, theft of cars, burglary, robbery, and criminal damage. The public toilets are specifically designed to discourage drug dealing.

The Trafford Centre generates 400 tonnes of waste a week.

There is a Jurassic *Jura Grey* limestone with ammonite and belemnite fossils in a column outside 'Mango' in Regent Crescent. The stone is from southern Germany and at 150 million years old was contemporary with the dinosaurs. It is unlikely that another out-of-town centre of such a size as the Trafford Centre will be built again in Britain. **PP**

The expensive view from Barton Bridge - This is one of the few places in Britain where you can look down on £1.6bn of real estate controlled by one man – John Whittaker, Chairman and main shareholder in Peel Holdings, which owns the extensive Bridgewater Estate with its Canal, the Trafford Centre, Chat Moss (soon to be developed too).

Peel also owns the Manchester Ship Canal, which connects it neatly to another possession – Liverpool John Lennon Airport. It resides, naturally, in the Peel Dome of the Trafford Centre. Peel is the largest private landowner in the North West with 12,500 acres, and earns £90mn of rental income a year.

This is big 'people business': the Trafford Centre sees 26 million visitors a year; Liverpool John Lennon Airport a further two million passengers a year. Nearby, the Imperial War Museum and the Lowry have all benefited from Peel Holdings' generosity – but also draw people into the area. A racecourse at Chat Moss will be the crowning glory. The M60 Motorway makes all this possible.

Junctions 12 and 13, with their overcrowding and propensity for shunts, will make it difficult.

Peel also plays a key role in the 'Ship Canal Corridor'. At the Manchester end, Peel has aspirations to develop Salford and Trafford into the 'the little Venice of the North West.' At the Liverpool end, it is running a competitor airport to Manchester's along with its Estuary Commerce Park. There is a strong feel of 'Monopoly' board portfolios here.

The original raison d'être of the Ship Canal in the 1890s was of course to allow Manchester's cotton barons to by-pass the Liverpool Docks Board's exorbitant tolls on imports of raw cotton from

abroad. The scale of the canal was ambitious – when first built there were only five vessels in the world too big to use it. The Ship Canal never however quite fulfilled its original role: intended to facilitate the export of Manchester's cotton goods in the depression of the 1880s, it saw instead a boom in the export to the British Empire and China of cotton looms. This export of looms took the jobs too: it was ultimately to undercut the leading role of Lancashire in textiles by the 1920s and 1930s. After all, Manchester had no discernible economic advantage in textiles (apart from its miserably damp climate which stopped the threads snapping) – it didn't grow any cotton, and its labour was no longer cheap. But the Ship Canal consolidated Manchester's other role – in the import and distributive sector, for grain, meat, oil and fruit, with knock-on effects in haulage. The number of Manchester carriers doubled to over 150 in the period 1894 to 1914.

The losers were Liverpool and Preston, which saw their distributive trade slip away. By 1910 Manchester,

a good 35 miles from any sea, was the fourth port of Britain. The Ship Canal helped make Trafford Industrial Park, with its string of famous names – Rolls Royce and Ford Motor Cars, Westinghouse, Kellogg's Cornflakes, Brooke Bond. Here too was based one far-sighted Mancunian: Alliott Verdon Roe of A.V.Roe, builder of the Vickers Vimy, the first aeroplane to fly the Atlantic in 1919; whose Spitfires may rightly be said to have saved Britain in 1940; and whose Lancaster Bombers destroyed so many German cities.

The Canal, like many engineering projects, came in at three times budget, costing some 15mn to build in 1894 – the equivalent of £1.2 bn. today. It had to be bailed out twice by Manchester Corporation (with ratepayers' money) for a total of £10mn (£770 mn), and took 30 years to pay for itself. Eventually, in the 1960s, containerisation and a shift in Shell's oil operations saw the end of its viability.

But it continued to stymie traffic, with huge jams

Above: The Bridgwater Canal passes over the Manchester Ship Canal. The Barton Canal bridge on the Bridgewater Canal over the Manchester Ship Canal rotates to allow ships to pass along the Manchester Ship Canal.

building up at the only crossing point at Barton Swing Bridge, whenever this was closed to allow ships to pass. The Barton High Level Bridge, begun in April 1957, was the solution. As you look down from the new Barton Bridge, with its huge piles of steel and concrete, you may like to know that in 1894 the Ship Canal banks re reinforced with woven willow in bundles, called 'fascines' – a peculiarly latinate mediaeval touch. The Viaduct also sits on a brook – the Salteye Brook – this is now part of the old course of the Irwell – its name betrays the fact that the Irwell was tidal and salty up to the 'eye' or island at this point.

The Ship Canal can be a vector for plants as well as humans and cargoes: note the steady incursion along its banks of the umbellifer, Giant Hog Weed, (Heracleum mantegazzianum) the Triffid plant from Asia which grows to five meters (16 feet), producing hundreds of viable seedlings, and whose mere touch provokes violent rashes, asthma and blinding migraine. Ineradicable and hostile: pretty, artless,

witless Nature looking after herself. Coming shortly to central Manchester. The authorities are conducting chemical warfare against it – black dead muck marks the spot. It is hard to see how this battle can ever be won – Japanese Knotgrass, Himalayan Impatience, not to mention invasive Victorian Rhododendrons, have all beaten us back. Pray that GM plants – perhaps maize coming up the canal from the US – do not hybridise with these invasive and noxious survivors.

The area below Barton Bridge gives striking views of a concentration of sewage works and filter beds on both the Peel Green (Northeast) and Davyhulme (Southwest) sides. There is a very good reason for this. Manchester Corporation chose to put its sewage works at Davyhulme in the early 1890s because of the proximity of the Manchester Ship Canal (as a recipient of treated sewage) and the absence of inhabitants at the time. The sewage works enabled the introduction of flush toilets into the City, and the gradual abolition of privies. These were in most cases pits full of ashes from domestic

coalfires, requiring emptying by hand. These cesspits, of which there were nearly 150,000 in Manchester, easily contaminated the water table. It may be worthwhile quoting the foul situation as Engels saw it in Manchester in 1844:

[These houses are] "the most horrible dwellings which I have yet beheld. In one of these courts there stands directly at the entrance, at the end of the covered passage, a privy without a door, so dirty that the inhabitants can pass into and out of the court only by passing through foul pools of stagnant urine and excrement. ...Below it on the river there are several tanneries which fill the whole neighbourhood with the stench of animal putrefaction. ...The first court below Ducie Bridge,

known as Allen's Court, was in such a state at the time of the cholera that the sanitary police ordered it evacuated, swept, and disinfected with chloride of lime... At the bottom flows, or rather stagnates, the Irk, a narrow, coal-black, foul-smelling stream, full of debris and refuse, which it deposits on the shallower right bank.

In dry weather, a long string of the most disgusting, blackish-green, slime pools are left standing on this bank, from the depths of which bubbles of miasmatic gas constantly arise and give forth a stench unendurable even on the bridge, forty or fifty feet above the surface of the stream. But besides this, the stream itself is checked every few paces by high weirs, behind which slime and refuse accumulate and rot in

a series of experiments in sewage treatment, first with chemical precipitation and land filtration followed by filter bed, until in 1904 Davyhulme finally invented the 'activated sludge process' which now lies, so to speak, at the bottom of all sewage treatment worldwide, and where Manchester has once again led the way.

Sewage treatment is not a bed of roses: in the 1980s during the construction of the M63 (now M60) some 35,000 cubic yards of sewage had to be removed from its site in Cheadle (presumably not solid enough to lay tarmac on) and re-deposited at salubrious Altrincham. There is a strange feeling of alienation to think of all that raw DNA material being transported around Cheshire, but doubtless there was a higher logic at work. At least it suggests one solution to the problem of where the Cloaca Maxima of the sleeping Goddess of Manchester may be located. PP

thick masses. Above the bridge are tanneries, bone mills, and gasworks, from which all drains and refuse find their way into the Irk, which receives further the contents of all the neighbouring sewers and privies."

1844 was in fact the year that Manchester passed its Borough Police Act, requiring that no new house be built without running water and an indoor toilet – the first such act in Britain. There followed the building of 95 miles of main sewers, and 148 miles of smaller feeders. The eventual removal by sewers of ordure from Manchester proper to Davyhulme must be applauded, even if the odour still lingers there. From the 1890s Davyhulme had the raw material for

Above: Construction of the
Barton High Level Bridge in 1957.
een approaching its end.

Left: Barton Swing Bridge (Bridgewater Canal). When the Bridgwater Canal was first built, it crossed the River Irwell at this point by an aqueduct. Later, the construction of the Manchester Ship Canal called for a solution which would allow ocean-going vessels to reach Manchester. The Barton Swing Bridge, (top) was the answer.

Above: Himalayan Immigrant Himalayan Balsam or Noli-me-tangere (Impatiens Glandulifera, an invasive sweet- smelling plant, along the course of the Ouzel Brook at M60 Junction 7, looking southwest on 7th July 2003.

ust Typical - Junction 11 has little to recommend it, except that it is typical of the land use of the M60: the Motorway is dropped between the quick and the dead: Eccles Sewage Works and Eccles Cemetery, while a little to the west s Barton Aerodrome on Barton Moss, and Boysnope Golf Course and Driving Range. There is also a car-breakers yard with fierce dogs, if you know where to look.

Here, in a hopeless morass of dumped building waste and old canals, week-end motorbike scramblers churn through the mud.

A little further, on the A57, is one of the largest collections of pallets in the world. Blue plastic pallets, meters high, hundreds of meters long, like some weird piece of installation art. Next to a giant Macro.

Impossibly blue, these pallets run for several hundred meters along the A57, from Junction 11. **PP**

ght: Mountain of Blue Pallets

eside the A57

The Manchester Ship Canal: *Technical Specifications*

Left: The Manchester Ship Canal. This 1990 view, looking east into Manchester, shows Barton Lock in the foreground, Barton High Level Bridge further on, and beyond that the original Barton Road) Bridge and the Swing Canal) Bridge. To the south is Dumplington Sewage Works, to the North that at Eccles. The still empty site of Trafford Centre 996) is visible at the top right. dead arm of the old River well can be seen at the left as dark green line

Original Estimated Cost: £5.25 mn, (£400 mn in 2004 terms). It had 39,000 shareholders – the largest number in a company to that date. The cheque for the purchase of the navigation rights was £1.7mn (£130 mn) – the largest ever written to that date.

Actual Cost: £15 mn, of which £1mn on labour (£1.2bn and £77 mn in 2004 terms – the Channel Tunnel of 31 miles cost some £21bn in 1994).

Cost of the land: The Canal originally required some 4495 acres (1,819 hectares), and cost £777,000 or £173 an acre. Prior to approval, the land was worth only £20-£30 an acre.

Project Contractor: Thomas Walker – he had built the Severn Tunnel for the Great Western Railway Company.

Machinery: 75 steam excavators, 124 steam cranes, and seven earth dredgers with 6,300 railway wagons.

Earnings: The Ship Canal was earning £500,000 a year by 1908, when total investment was some £17mn – it was only paying about 3% return. The payback period in effect stretched into the 1930s.

Original Depth: 26 feet (7.9 m) – built to be the same as the Suez Canal

Final Depth: 30 feet (9.1 m)

Length: 35 miles (56.8 km.)

Rise: The Canal lifts vessels some 60 ft 6 in. (18.4 m)

DWT: Ships of up to 400 tons in 1894.

Begun: 11th November 1887 – First turf cut by Lord Egerton of Tatton.

Opened: 1st January 1894.

Official Opening: 21st May 1894 by Queen Victoria from the Royal Yacht 'Enchantress'.

Navvies: Shanty villages were built (e.g. at Acton Grange) to house the 16,000 labourers – called 'navvies' or 'navigators.'

First Official Vessel: The 'Norseman' Steam Yacht, owned by Samuel Platt

First Official Steam Vessel: The 'Pioneer' Wholesale Co-operative Cargo Carrier:

Locks: The original five sets remain: Eastham, Latchford, Irlam, Barton and Mode Wheel.

Bridges: The original seven swing road bridges remain, though Trafford Road no longer rotates. There are four high level road bridges and five high level railway viaducts (Cadishead and Latchford are disused). **PP**

Above: Barton Aerodrome. Light aircraft lined up on the apron at Barton Aerodrome with the north slope of the Barton Bridge visible behind.

Chat Moss & Worsley: *World Heritage Site - "The stretch of motorway between Junction 12 and 13 (Worsley to Eccles junction) is the busiest stretch of motorway in the country outside of the M25. It has an annual average weekday traffic flow of approximately 185,000 vehicles with peak hour flows exceeding the recommended flows for this standard of road by 34%.*

The dominance of major roads in the area means that the entire area suffers from poor air quality, high levels of noise pollution and severe traffic congestion. The area is of great historic significance, particularly in terms of its industrial heritage. The Bridgewater Canal, opened in 1761, was the first canal in England to be constructed independently of a natural stream. Further, Worsley Delph is the entrance to an extensive network of underground canals linking the canal to the coalfields of the area. The significance of this has been recognised in the potential application for World Heritage Site status and in turn gives the area tourism potential."

This quotation is from the *'City of Salford, Worsley and Boothstown Area Plan – A Vision for the next 10-20 Years'*

So, The M60 is a problem child at this point – crowded and dangerous, and likely to become more so if Peel Holdings and world tourism have their way. Daniel Defoe, passing through in the 1720s, saw the area of Chat Moss very differently: 'Black and dirty, frightful to think of, for it will bear neither Horse nor Man...' He believed the overwhelmed pre-glacial pines that rose in Chat Moss from time to time were still alive and growing in the sump. He was of course mistaken: at 7000 years old, this ice-age mess of peat, pine and bog pre-dates Creation, as then imagined.

These strange lands, a blanket of glacial deposits and peat mosses, generated their own folklore: the Green Boggart, Jinny Greenteeth, Jack o' Lantern, all threatened benighted travellers in their own malignant fashion. Strange flickering lights and voices from the dark bogs drew people to a watery death. Until at last canals and improvements drained away their habitat, and the spirits faded sighing into the earth once more, or withdrew to remoter wildernesses such as Boggart Hole Clough.

If it is true that Manchester is built on cotton, it took a Northumbrian engineer, George Stephenson, to float a railway in 1830 on brushwood over this bottomless bog. Here the Liverpool & Manchester's track on its herringbone base of piles still rises and falls to the beat of the trains, with the rhythm rippling out across the Moss – and has the curious distinction of inspiring a piece of modern music by Sir Peter Maxwell Davies, now the Master of the Queen's Music. The Railway's opening is said to have put 30 stagecoaches out of business – but tripled passengers into Manchester via Liverpool Road Station to 1600 a day. Built with Liverpudlian money, it succeeded in reinforcing Liverpool merchants' hold on cotton imports: Mancunians owned only 2% if its share capital. The railway's success can be seen as one of the eventual instigators for Mancunian merchants to build the Manchester Ship Canal.

This has always been an abandoned isolated area – even its place-names betray it – 'Botany Bay Wood' was, in the grim humour of the Lancashire farm labourer, a place on the other side of the world. Or 'Hephzibah' – a weak and surprisingly common biblical joke from Isaiah – 'no longer shall your land be called desolate'. Convenient, though. It was here in 1947 that the much-loved Belle Vue Zoo Elephant 'Lil' was unsentimentally hidden on her demise and left to rot – until her excarnated whitened bones were ready for collection for the Manchester Museum. But this is an old tradition – Celtic Worsley Man was executed here two millennia ago, probably a victim, like Merlin and Cheshire's better known Lindow Man, of the

An Elephant Ride

violent triple death – brained, garroted and drowned.

Yet the lonely, lovely character of Chat Moss is unexpected, so close to Manchester and the M60. This vast expanse betrays its origins as a huge sump by its level nature. It looks like admirable cycling country, but the open lanes are confusing, rapidly deteriorate into dirt tracks, and peter out at the edge of the brown fields, or at police access points to the motorway. Indeed, Chat Moss probably keeps its isolated nature because it is bounded by two motorways (the M60 to the east, the M62 to the south), the rust-coloured Bridgewater Canal to the north, and the East Lancs Road to the west.

At first sight the land is featureless – huge unhedged prairie fields of wheat and potatoes, over which pass wind and clouds ceaselessly. But then you begin to notice the deep drainage ditches, where a man might walk unseen, the stands of reed mace, and the small pools with grey herons – showing how hard won this land was from the bogland. In June the countryside gives itself slowly, in very English fashion – heady wayside stands of elder in flower, foxgloves, comfrey, sticky burr, small groups of beehives. Here are pheasants, skylarks, long-tailed tits, and the occasional buzzard feeling awkwardly for the thermals. All five owl species breed here, silently hunting up and down these prairies in the darkness, while Nightjars churr in their last wilderness. Then you become aware that the long miles of Botany Bay Wood have silently crept up to embrace you – impenetrable old reddish pine plantations to one side, and rhododendron, beech and birch, tangled with ferns and briars, to the other.

This landscape is unlike anything else locally. It lacks the rural fussy prettiness of Cheshire, or the ruggedness of Lancashire. Its nearest relative is Lindow Moss – but Chat Moss lacks the bittiness of Lindow and the rough tenements of its squatters. One might have said Ashton Moss, but that has now vanished under the developers' juggernauts and piledrivers. Here the bluebrick farms are far apart, and in a changing light the landscape can look as brooding and abandoned as the fens. Small wonder that the defeated poet Michael Drayton visited it in 1600. The female spirit of Chat Moss Vale is inscribed on his map of Lancashire, seated on a bank of peat turves: *Great Chatmosse Lyes full of Turfe, and Marle, her unctuous Minerall, And Blocks as blacke as Pitch (with boring-Augurs found). There at the general Flood supposed to be drownd.*

Utilitarian Defoe had a very different view of Chat Moss: 'What nature meant by such a useless production, 'tis hard to imagine.' But Chat Moss may not be the local name for much longer: just as Dumplington became Trafford Centre country, this is now to be Salford Forest Park. Chat Moss is largely owned by Peel Holdings, and has been the subject of bitter and hard-fought planning disputes in the last few years. In October 1998 Peel Estates proposed large-scale development of the land south of the Bridgewater canal and west of the M60 Junction 12. Their 'vision' includes the opening up of the land to wider public access with trails, play areas and visitor centres in Botany Bay Wood and on the present farmland between the wood and the canal.

The proposal would mark the end for Malkins Wood Farm, since it is planned to build a new horse-racing

course on the land. It would be a major project that would involve the construction of a new access road to the site from the East Lancashire Road to the north.

The proposed new racecourse would be both flat and jump racing, with a grandstand for 6,000 and space for 20,000 at 30 major events a year. There would be an equestrian centre and stabling for 100 horses. Plus the trimmings: golf course, naturally, children's play area, an hotel with ecovillage (chalet-style) accommodation and a new canalside pub. Meanwhile, just on the other side of the ship canal, plans have been unveiled for a £60m scheme to build a new 20,000-capacity stadium for Salford Reds Rugby League Club, along with a four star hotel, a casino and another shopping mall.

Junction 12, where the M62 and M60 intersect, is however, an accident blackspot with higher than national average rates, abetted by steep gradients, narrow lanes and a concentration of 'lane weaving' manoeuvres by frustrated motorists. Indeed, peak time shunts are the major form of incident here. These are perhaps built into the M60: the large number of closely sited junctions are designed to allow traffic to disperse quickly into local rat runs. Perhaps fast horses are the answer for the M60, but not in the way currently envisaged for Chat Moss. **PP**

eft: Elephant at Belle Vue Zoo, 900s. Lil was left to the lements on Chat Moss

ight: Liverpool to Manchester ailway at Chat Moss, 1830. Stephenson's undulating line for he Liverpool to Manchester ailway across Chat Moss. This vas the first intercity railway in he world.

Above: A panorama of Chat
Moss. Looking west towards
Chat Moss taken from the slip
road at Junction 13, Worsley.
In the lower left is the
Bridgewater Canal. This area
may soon become a hive of
activity and development.

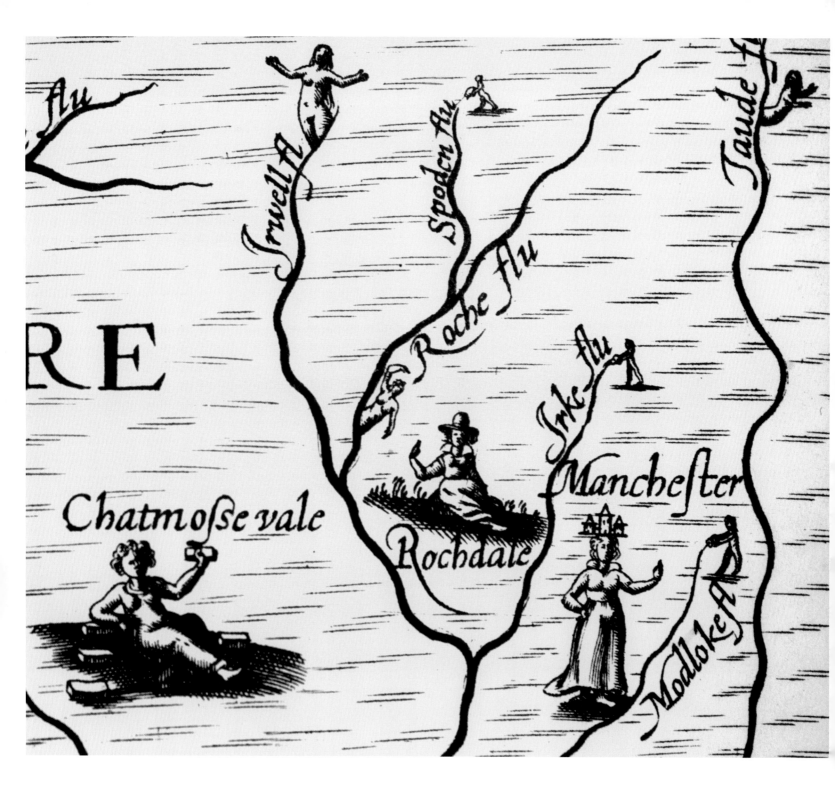

Above: The Spirit of Chat Moss.
Seated on a bed of turves,
c. 1600. Nearby is the City of
Manchester, with hat. From
Michael Drayton's curious
Polyolbion

Worsley - Worsley is signalled to the orbiting motorist going north by the spire of St Mark's Church rising from dense woodland, visible to the left early on from the height of Barton High Level Bridge. Even at a glimpse it looks grand, aristocratic, expensive. Listed Grade I in 2004, it was begun in 1846 by Sir Gilbert Scott, and here are buried all the notable Egertons, owners of stately Worsley Hall and Tatton Hall, Earls of Ellesmere, and now extinct. Gone to earth, just above their rich coal seams.

Worsley, literally cut in half by the motorway – a bad case of 'severance' in motorway jargon – was one of the most remarkable of all the aristocratic estates of England, thanks to Francis Egerton, Duke of Bridgewater (1736-1803), among the greatest entrepreneurs of the industrial revolution. Possessed of great underground riches in the form of a hill full of coal under his Worsley New Hall estate, and knowing of the insatiable need for fuel in the city of Manchester, he was faced with three problems:

how to drain the mines of water, how to extract the coal, and how to get the coal to Manchester.

Who came up with the brilliant solution to all three problems simultaneously, whether the Duke himself or his indefatigable agent John Gilbert, is hard to know. 'Soughs' or drains bored horizontally into the hill to drain out the water were an old idea; making the soughs navigable so that boats could be floated in and loaded direct from the coal face was a daring

move. Continuing the waterway as an artificial canal all the way into Manchester, including an aqueduct – water over water, crossing the River Irwell at Barton – must have seemed like madness. Pushing the line all the way down to Runcorn and Merseyside was a stroke of genius – it connected Manchester to New Orleans and its cotton. Or at least Runcorn to Dublin: Irish pigs were shipped by canal to Stretford, kept in makeshift wooden styes, then slaughtered and salted, providing bacon for Manchester's industrial workers.

James Brindley was the brilliant, homespun mechanic who dreamed up the canal techniques: literally. He was pretty well illiterate, but when faced with a problem he would go to bed (he lived at Worsley Old Hall) and not get up until it was all worked out in his head. In this case, the underground ramps and cranes, the puddling with clay to make the canal watertight, the famous Barton Aqueduct, and the warehouses and flood controls at Castlefield in Manchester. The Duke was the driving force, the one who put at risk the whole of his vast estates – but without selling a

single acre. Gilbert was the one who made it happen, finding the navvies and the materials.

The Duke was only 22 in 1758, the date of the successful bill in parliament which enabled the canal to be built, allowing compulsory purchase of the land over which it had to pass. By the time the first coals arrived in Manchester he was in his late twenties, and virtually bankrupt, but the mines and canal recouped the outlay and the effort triumphantly, paying £24,000 a year at the time of his death (about £2 mn today). He died childless, but his adopted son, Francis Leveson-Gower kept the Egerton name going – but it died out a second time in 1958, this time for good.

What remains of all this enterprise? The Duke's cut, the Bridgewater canal, still carries plenty of boats on its orange ochreous waters (full of iron hydroxide flowing out from the mines) and the decision to name Manchester's new concert venue The Bridgewater Hall proves that he is not forgotten, as does Duke's 92, the public house named after the 92nd lock on the canal at Castlefield. Here at Worsley the village still retains to a surprising degree the well-ordered ambience of an estate village, laid out on generous lines with plenty of greenery and picturesque cottages.

Its present desirability does not tell of the busy industrial scene it would have presented under the first Duke, when the Green was the works yard and the fountain was a steam engine chimney. In the middle of the village is the mysterious Delph, that old word for Adam digging, the dim declivity of dappled shade where it all started. There in the water lies a 'starvationer', one of the canal boats, with thin protruding ribs, by which men lying on their backs walked the Duke's coal out of the labyrinthine tunnels. Dismal diggings, dangerous depths, dark dungeons of doom.

The underground canals were a huge tourist attraction in their day, one of the wonders of the world. Even today anyone who can say that they went down there before it was all sealed up in 1968, is something of a local celebrity. There is talk that, methane permitting, their 42 miles of tunnel, reaching four miles up to Farnworth, near Bolton, will acquire World Heritage status and re-open to take their rightful place in the history of the Industrial Revolution in Manchester and the world.

On the other side of the M60 motorway is the stately domain with its halls, gardens and rolling acres – what is left of them. Worsley Old Hall still stands, a pub, prettily if unconvincingly timber-framed and surrounded by a golf course. It once had a courtyard but that has been infilled. On a line due south of it was the Brick Hall, a handsome if plain mansion of about 1750. Sullied by an unfortunate suicide, it was knocked down in 1846 to make way for a third hall. Worsley New Hall and St Mark's church were both built in the 1840s for another Francis Egerton, the second Earl of Ellesmere.

The hall, a pompous Elizabethan pile designed by Edward Blore, has gone, like so many pompous piles. A 1950s concrete bunker, relic of the Cold War, sits in its cellars. The garden with its elaborate terracing, lake, grottoes and ice-house is still there under the dank overgrowth. So is the walled garden with its decorative head-gardener's house; indeed it is in use as a garden centre. Beyond is an astonishing swathe of empty country stretching to Leigh and Irlam. The church and vicarage remain – they are both of course by the top architect of the day, Sir Gilbert Scott.

Fletcher Moss of Didsbury visited Worsley in 1912, travelling from Manchester in the famous 1851 State Barge (see illustrations) drawn by horses with postillions in livery – lucky man – and then legged round the underground tunnels in a 'starvationer'. Perhaps we should allow him the last word:

'I still buy my coal from "the Duke's". The price does exceed the fourpence per hundredweight they were bound not to exceed: now it is a shilling and a ha'penny. It is good coal, burning steadily away with very little ash. It is tumbled into the boats at Worsley, miles away from the light of day, floated to Stretford, carted here, gives a cheerful warmth, and his Lordship allows me thruppunce ha'penny off if I pay in a week: and a contented mind is great riches.' MH

Above: Worsley Delph: Once a place of industry, the canal is now used by waterway enthusiasts. The brown colour of the water comes from metal deposits in the mines (delves), which are entered by the canal at this point.

Right: St Mark's Worsley From the level fields of Chat Moss, the M60 Motorway curves up and round to pass in front of St Mark's Church by Sir Gilberts Scott at Worsley, Junction 13. Buried in the Church are the last of the Egertons.

Left: Worsley Green. Mist in the atmosphere has reduced the sun's brightness to that of the moon. On the left is The Tower, monument to the Duke of Bridgewater. Worsley Village has some 40 listed buildings.

Above: Cobbelstones on Bridgewater Canal Bridge. humpback bridge over the Bridgewater Canal at Worsley. They were intended to give purchase for the barge tow horses. Posts added more recently prevent cars from mounting the bridge.

Ever Vigilant: *Do you need specs on the M60?* - Although there are as yet no redcap traffic wardens on the M60, there are innumerable other ways to be observed and penalised. To drive on it is to subscribe both to the Motorway rules of the Highway Code and also to a secret unwritten code: you agree implicitly to be watched by police CCTV and speed cameras, to be counted by Highway Agency automatic traffic counters, and to be warned by MIDAS – the Motorway Incident Detection and Automatic Signalling which usually flashes up the depressing 'Queues after next Jcn.' message.

The internet is alive with tales that the gantries of the M60 are to be fitted with the SPECS speed cameras. SPECS does exist: it is a computer-camera system. As you pass a SPECS digital camera, it reads your registration number. When you go past the next SPECS camera, your number plate is read again. The computer 'knows' how far apart the cameras are, so it can work out your average speed. The system is fully automatic, and issues speeding ticket without any form of human intervention.

These cameras do not flash. They work 24/7, 365 days a year, and theoretically, there's absolutely no limit on the number of tickets that the system can issue. In a trial run, the Manchester Police Central Ticket Office processed 2,500 offences in 6 man-hours, which is a lot of £80 revenue in fines (£200k actually). With a rapid accumulation of penalty points, you could lose your licence in a few short miles on one journey between a round of golf at Didsbury, and a quick run up to JJB Golf Centre at the Trafford Centre. It is said that the system is set to fire at 78 mph, which should capture most of the UK motorway drivers in any one year. In-car radar detectors are no protection against SPECS, as it is entirely passive: there is no radar or laser beam to detect.

More alarmingly, the 'computer' knows where your car (and implicitly you) are at any one moment. Real Big Brother, or is this just an internet urban myth ?

Of the three classic defences if sent a speeding summons in the post, two were invented here: first, the Cheshire local 'Neil and Christine Hamilton.' This requires two people to be in the car, neither of whom can remember who was driving. Be careful if you use this defence: the latest CCTV cameras have Facial Recognition Systems which can process 1000 faces an hour. Second, the 'Granny' defence requires the car to be registered in your granny's name, and costs you a grand for her non-appearance at court. She also collects your penalty points. And the 'Dwight Yorke' football defence requires your agent, if you have one, to send in your reply – unsigned.

The amusing part in all this attention to speed is that speeding is only implicated in about 7% of road accidents – drink driving (not yet remotely detectable, but who knows), is a far more serious factor. And the Transport Research Laboratory is conducting tests on the effects of Cannabis – with state of the art driving simulators and, presumably, state of the art spliffs. Motorways are relatively safe places – only 3 to 5% of chillingly named KSI incidents ('killed and seriously injured') take place on motorways – about 1500 in a bad year.

But the M60 is not alone in its remote surveillance: since late 2003 visitors to the Trafford Centre are having their vehicle details scanned by Automatic Number Plate Recognition (ANPR) 'to detect and locate people and vehicles of interest to Greater Manchester Police'. This is described as a joint partnership between the public and private sector. The system has involved the installation of 13 covert cameras, fitted with infra-red capability to allow scanning in the hours of darkness.

The system identifies stolen vehicles or those listed as wanted for a variety of crimes: 'Within seconds the registration of the vehicle is checked against a series of local intelligence databases, confidential police records and the Police National Computer (PNC) controlled from Stretford Operational Policing Unit. If the vehicle is listed as stolen, or as being associated with any type of crime, the Centre's control room is raised'. About 77,000 vehicles were examined over the first trial weekend, of which 600 were in contravention of the Road Traffic Act in some way – perhaps just having been clocked speeding to the Trafford Centre.

For some, these developments are welcome and reassuring – after all, iris scanning is now being introduced at Manchester Airport to cut terrorism. Some people look to the future and shudder. For those with hoods up and baseball caps down, the next piece of software will identify 'gait' – the way you walk. Or possibly the way you drive. Take off that ridiculous mask. PP

Wardley Hall & the Screaming Skull - Wardley is invisible from the motorway, but it is perilously close to the biggest intersection of the entire ring, the composite made up the M60 Junctions 14 and 15 and the M61 Junctions 1 and 2. The Hall, on in a little green island, is jammed in between this great interchange and the East Lancs Road, the A580. So from the map it looks highly unpromising.

Photographs lower expectations further: a low house of dark red brick with a few timber-framed bits at the back. And yet we know it is deeply historical, and especially famous as 'The House of the Skull'.

Fletcher Moss was not expecting much either, when he visited the place in 1905. 'The reader shall not be troubled with any description of the miserable grimy streets of Salford. In a few miles we came to higher ground, with fewer houses, but the people were no cleaner. A badly-worn paved road led through a blackened land dotted with coal-pits, or mills, overhung with a dull pall of smoke, through which the shrieking engines and the clanging trams rushed their hideous way. The abomination of desolation brooded over all.'

But preconceptions are immediately laid aside, then as now, on turning into the leafy drive, past the pretty timber-framed lodge and into the front garden with its circle of springy turf. Fletcher Moss had the same experience: 'an end came to our depression when we turned a corner and suddenly found ourselves before a bit from another century, or another county, standing alone as it were forgotten and forlorn'. There in front of us lies the hall, not pretty it is true,

but with a tantalising glimpse through the gate of a delicious courtyard. Off to one side is a nice stable yard, perhaps eighteenth century; and can we hear chickens skrawking?' When Fletcher Moss visited, the house had reverently been rescued from terminal decay by the Earl of Ellesmere. Since 1930 it has been the private residence of the Roman Catholic Bishop of Salford.

The house is built around a small irregular courtyard. Not many are left like this – Speke is the best known in our area. Hopwood is another, and there is the little cloister at Chetham's. Come to think of it, there is a courtyard at Dunham too, and Lyme, but they are on a grander scale. Often the courtyard has been opened

out, as at Bramall and Smithills. Maybe they were dank in winter and the flags got green and slippery. Here at Wardley though, on a spring day, the courtyard is especially good, preserving its timber-framing on three sides, trapping the sun, and shutting out the noise of the M60 Motorway.

On stepping inside it is soon clear that the house is a good deal better preserved than expected, in fact inside its brick outer casing the sixteenth century house is virtually complete. The quadrangle is very irregular – how is it that our ancestors could never build straight round four sides of a rectangle? The question every architectural historian will ask is – did it once have an open great hall, like Smithills or

Previous: Photo series showing heavy goods vehicles crossing Simister Island Interchange bot on the mid-level motorway roundabout and on the top leve bridge. The images were capture on 1 August 2003 between 1.09 (red Transamerica Leasing) and 1.37 (White B&Q). Straight on under the bridge, the M66 motorway extends north towar Rawtenstall. To the left is the north west section of the M60 (formerly part of the M62) and the right, the M62 towards Halifax, Leeds and Hull. In the distance are the hills above Ramsbottom.

Left: Wardley Hall. House of the Skull, now the official residenc of the Roman Catholic Bishop Salford. It stands next to the M60 at Wardley, just north of th East Lancs Road.

Right: The Skull of Ambrose Barlow, Catholic, executed 10 September 1641.

Ordsall? Pevsner in his magisterial 'Buildings of England' says yes. This architectural historian says no. The evidence is to be found in the upper hall, where the intermediate floor rests on a neat moulding built into the frame. The floor supports cannot be a later modification because they are part of the structure. So the intermediate floor is original. Wardley was an up-to-date house, not an old fashioned one, built for comfort rather than for outmoded ideas of feudal living, with a modest single-storey hall below and a pleasant draught-free chamber above.

Halfway up the stairs is a hole in the wall, visible on both sides but sealed with glass. Inside the hole is The Skull. Who is it? There have been doubts. For a while he was identified as a ne'er-do-well son of the family, Roger Downes, but now he is venerated as Ambrose Barlow, Catholic martyr and, since 1970, saint. Although the skull has been lost and found a couple of times there is no reason to doubt it. Ambrose was christened Edward Barlow in 1585 in Barlow Hall near Chorlton-cum-Hardy. That is another under-researched old house, another that once had a courtyard, and another that is not far from the M60 (Junction 5). He studied abroad at Douay and Valladolid (Dr. Dee, Astrologer Royal and Master of Manchester College, lent him a Spanish Grammar), made his vow as a Benedictine when he took the name Ambrose, and was ordained priest two years later. He returned to England, and ministered secretly to the Lancashire Catholics.

Four times he was arrested and four times released, but finally in 1641, having decided not to abandon his flock before Easter and thus breaking new penal laws, he was arrested at Leigh, tried at Lancaster castle, and sentenced to die by that most barbaric of ceremonious deaths, 'hanged, dismembered, disemboweled, quartered, and boiled in tar'; but as another martyr cheerfully observed, 'all this is but one death'. His head was raised on a pike at the

Collegiate Church in Manchester (now the cathedral) for all to see and be frightened by. Somehow it was eventually rescued, hidden, and found its way to Wardley where it was buried for a while under the dairy floor. Now it rests, as we have seen halfway up the stairs. If it should ever leave the hall frightful disturbances will ensue, storms will rage, chimneys fall, spirits wail. So runs the tale.

Having explored the house, the setting and geography of the place can be assessed. It is difficult to understand because its world ends immediately to the west with the bank of the M60 Motorway. There is a moat, unusually wide and unusually round rather than square. It has been partly filled in which is pity, but still makes a romantic setting to the south and west. A deep clough runs by the hall, so the moat needed quite a high dam. The original settlement – who knows when – must have been on a tongue of land defended by two steep river valleys. The hall grew up in instalments, its sides aligned with the cloughs not with each other. Extra defenses were made, culminating in the moat with its dam. Now the impassable M60 provides almost perfect seclusion, though not quiet. **MH**

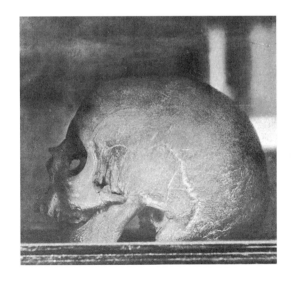

The River Irwell: *Angry, Perverse and Wandering* - The River Irwell rises as a spring in a field on Irwell Farm, north of Bacup in Lancashire and in theory runs 30 miles (48 km) to join the Mersey, as its most important tributary, at Irlam, though by here it has already become the Manchester Ship Canal.

A puzzling name, according to the expert, Ekwall. He favoured the Old English 'irre': an angry, perverse and wandering current. And wander it does, in loopy signatures through Salford and Manchester. In the north the M60 crosses it at Clifton (Junction 16), where the country below is surprisingly wild and abandoned. In the South the M60 passes over it again just before Junction 11 on the Barton Viaduct –the Irwell has by then picked up the River Medlock but the names of both streams are by now extinguished in the Manchester Ship Canal. But they have a quiet revenge: every year they deposit nearly a million tonnes of silt onto the bed of the Canal, requiring constant dredging.

The Irwell sweeps up most of the other local rivers – The Roch, which rises near Todmorden and runs some twelve miles (19 km.) past Rochdale, joins it near to Bury; the Irk, from near Royton joins the Irwell at Manchester; and the Medlock, which rises near Oldham as well as lesser streams such as the Cornbrook.

The total watershed of the Irwell is consequently some 170,000 acres giving a normal and controllable water flow of 370 tons per minute – about twice as much weight as cars on the Barton Bridge. But the Irwell in spate has in the past been a force of nature to be feared: in November 1866, swollen by heavy rains, its flow increased by around 113 times to 42,000

Left: Bridge over the River Irwell at Clifton by Junction 17. Junction 16 carrying the M60 (formerly M62) Motorway across the Irwell Valley. On the right an electricity pylon carrying power cables into Manchester from Ringley, once site of a power station.

tons per minute. Constricted by the narrowness of its throat through the sandstone cliffs between the Adelphi Weir (beyond Salford Crescent) and Manchester Cathedral, it flooded over 1000 acres, sweeping through Lower Broughton, Salford and neighbouring parts of Manchester, and causing some £5 mn of damage in today's prices.

In July 1872, another long spell of rain led to similar flooding, though with more macabre consequences. A month's rain fell in two days, and the unruly Medlock disinterred about 50 coffins from the Manchester City Cemetery, and swept them, along with the contents of a complete fabric works: boilers, dyes, 20,000 pieces of calico and the dead, all mixed indiscriminately and falling into the Irwell at Knott Mill near to Castlefield. Water was 15 feet deep in some areas, but, surprisingly, only one person died.

The Irwell was at this time an open sewer for domestic and industrial waste 'a nuisance and a discredit to the intelligence of Lancashire men' according to Corbett, who was borough engineer in Salford in the 1900s and wrote the classic history of the River. Refuse from the new-fangled gas works had begun the long decline in the 1840s – gaslight brought darkness to the river. It also received ash and cinder waste, and this, added to the excrement of bleach works, had killed the river dead by the 1880s: no plants were growing in it, or for a height of two feet, along its banks. Yet this was the river that until the 1820s was yielding salmon and snigs (eels), with grayling, chub and dace. It was then still drinkable at the steps below Manchester Cathedral. There followed of course 150 years of pollution and neglect.

The Irwell Sculpture Trail

But a quiet environmental miracle has happened in the last twenty years or so. The Irwell, famously filthy for so many years, has come clean. What is more, the Irwell valley has recovered something of the beauty that it must have had before the industrial revolution ruined it, seemingly forever. The Irwell is now navigable by tour boats, and there are even plans to create a beach upstream from Victoria Railway Station. Corbett would be proud.

To celebrate this, and to help to bring it about, the local authorities along its 33 mile course - Rossendale, Bury, Salford, have cooperated in the creation of the Irwell Valley Sculpture Trail. The idea is admirable. The commissioning authorities have not faltered. Money has flowed. The sad thing is that the Art is mostly lamentable. And the vandals have had a ball.

In the little marketplace at Ramsbottom is a giant tin amphora on its side forever trickling water into a grid. In the carpark at Burrs Country Park at Bury is a big silver mousetrap (tourist trap, geddit??). At Radcliffe an old railway bridge restored as a footbridge has gained fancy railings with birds and butterflies. Scrap merchants have resourcefully removed all the bronze bits.

Nearby are ten giant blocks of granite, imported at vast expense from Spain (is there no local stone, no British granite?). They are powerful, enigmatic. The vandals have attempted destruction in the only way possible, by stacking old mattresses and anything else burnable against the stones and firing them; great flakes of stone are cracked off by the intense heat. There is food for thought here. Casual vandalism against crap art is one thing, but when we see the attempted destruction of a fifteen ton block of granite by fire, something more serious is going on.

The granite-block work is titled 'Untitled'. The amphora is called 'Tilted vase'. These pieces have nothing to say, and they say it loud and clear. Maybe that gets up people's noses, especially in an area where great industries have come and gone and there is nothing to show for it. **MH**

Pilkington: *Extraordinary Tile Works* - Just below junction 16, rammed into an angle of the A666, the M60, the River Irwell, a railway and two canals is the Pilkington Tile Works, distinguishable by its large corrugated sheds covered in white powder.

The Pilkington Tile Works owes its location to a series of curious mis-haps: it sits near to where the Clifton and Kersley Coal Company was, in 1889, puzzling how best to deal with the large amounts of water in their new mine-shafts. The attempt to mine coal proved futile but the pit-owners, the four Pilkington Brothers, had noticed that the shafts produced large amounts of white clay or 'marl', and decided to turn their hand to glazed brick and tile-making. There appears then to have followed some high level poaching, with one William Burton being lured from Josiah Wedgwood in the Potteries. Burton was a skilled chemist, and went on to develop many of the glazes for the new company.

The Tile Works was finally established in 1892 as the Pilkington Tile and Pottery Company. Pottery manufacture ran until 1937 – small pottery wares, like buttons and hatpins but also vases purchased for decoration from other potteries. By 1903, the company had discovered an opalescent glaze that became popular as the Lancastrian pottery line. The Factory was hedging its bets in naming: located in Lancashire and itself called Lancastrian (Royal was added after a Royal Warrant was obtained) it also had a glaze called 'Cunian' – a shortening of Mancunian for Manchester.

But Pilkington's really found their market niche in the early 1900s with what they called Parian faïence, which they guaranteed "to stand exposure to the weather in our country, and which is so highly vitrified as to be unattackable by the sulphuric acid vapours in the air, and impermeable to soot or dust." Ideal for the grimy industrial North West.

They also seem to have looted the style books, with painted tiles designed by Lewis F. Day, inspired by the beautiful tile decoration of Persia, notably the city of Esfahan. The patterns are English enough in detail, but the colour schemes, of rich cobalt blue, sage green, bright turquoise, and Rhodian red are similar to those employed in the best Oriental work of the fifteenth and sixteenth centuries.

The tiles turn up in strange places: they cover the walls of the long-closed but soon to be restored Victoria Baths in Manchester with deep sea-green fronds; a war memorial at Ashton-under-Lyne; and with marine blue the bathrooms of the Titanic in its deep grave.

Beyond the Tile Works, the sudden and deep Irwell valley between Junction 15 and 17 is also not without its own interest: in the space of a few hundred meters the M60 passes under the A666 (surely the most ominously numbered road in Britain after the A13) and once an area, before motorway improvements, afflicted with so many accidents that it was known as 'Death Valley'. The Motorway then passes over the Irwell and Fletcher's Canal.

Here, to the left as you leave Junction 16 going east, is Clifton Marina, visible as a large body of water and the result of gravel extraction for the M62 (now M60) at this point. This is another spot where Brindley, the canal engineer has left his mark. The drainage of the aptly named Wet Earth Colliery had puzzled the best engineers in the County. In 1752 Brindley was called in, and decided he needed more power for bigger pumps. He first constructed a head of water at a weir to the north at nearby Ringley. The lie of the land dictated a channel some 800 yards long to a point opposite the colliery, but on the wrong side of the River Irwell. The water then plunged vertically into a tunnel under the Irwell. Contrary to expectations, it flowed through this great siphon and drove the pumps that drained the workings. Both drive water

and pumped water were then discharged back to the River Irwell. An elegant and simple solution, from a man both uncouth and illiterate.

The colliery has gone, leaving a jumble of shafts; the narrowboats only run for pleasure now. This is Country Park country. But this whole valley is in fact honeycombed with tunnels – nine feet high, hand-hacked through the sandstone by the light of tallow candles, dangerous when the Irwell is in spate, and still largely unexplored. **PP**

Forgetting: *Agecroft Hall* - How many memories can one place hold? Agecroft Hall, ancestral home of the Catholic-turned-Protestant Dauntseys, is a fourteenth century quadrangular structure, some 35 yards long on each wall, surrounded by a moat which doubles as a 'stew' or fish pond.

It has over 50 rooms, and the interior galleries around the courtyard, now covered, were originally open to the weather. Below the centre window on the upper storey is a badge – a white hart couchant, emblem of Richard II – murdered in 1399 and said to be the first casualty of the Wars of the Roses between the Houses of Lancaster and York. Here, if anywhere, is Lancashire memory.

Inside is a later window, showing a red rose and a white entwined, and dated 1485. It is inscribed 'H' (for Henry VII) and 'E' for Elizabeth of York, whose marriage united the Red Rose of Lancashire to the White of York, and extinguished the Wars. Eight wooden figures stand above the entrance to the

drawing room: salvaged from the pulpit of the private chapel, they represent War and Peace.

But this is not on the Irwell – this is on the James River, Richmond, Virginia, USA. Agecroft Hall fled to America in the 1920s, every wooden peg, plank and post removed, numbered and re-assembled.

The Hall had already narrowly avoided demolition in the 1840s when it lay in the path of the advancing Manchester to Bolton Railway line, only diverted at the last moment. By 1925 it was falling into final decay, surrounded by mining rubble, pinned between a railway and a canal, and liable to pit subsidence – 'a reproachful jewel in a ruined

Left: Agecroft Hall. As it was
before removal in the 1902s.
It can still be visited by the
James River in Virginia, USA,
or on the internet.

Above: Agecroft Power Station.

This haunting view shows

Agecroft Power Station in 1983

– solid and gigantic, dwarfing

human sporting activity. A

solitary white horse (lower left)

lends the scene a mythical air.

Above: Forest Bank Prison. On the Agecroft site, specialises in treating 'substance abuse.'

landscape' according to the Manchester Guardian. But rescue was at hand: Thomas C. Williams Jr. had the means and the interest to dismantle Agecroft, and to crate and transport it to Richmond, Virginia, where it still stands, on the banks of the James River. It has acquired extra patina: an Elizabethan Knot Garden and a Sunken Garden, filled with the appropriate exotica of Tradescant plants. But this was not the end for Agecroft, Lancashire.

England here and now should be the four white milk-bottle cooling towers and twin chimneys of the Agecroft Power Station, which was built in 1926 on the site of Agecroft Hall and was closed only in 1993, after the miners' strikes and Margaret Thatcher did for the domestic coal industry. Inconceivable that this vast cathedral to power has gone too.

No, Agecroft now is Forest Bank Prison, a £39 mn. Private Finance Initiative on the power station site.

1040 places for 18-20 year olds, privately run by UK Detention Services on a 25 year remit. A Training Centre for vocational and other courses: cookery, welding and substance abuse. A much praised Rough Guide printed in five languages is given to all new arrivals (but read aloud to them, just in case, by a literate warder). Forest Bank is owned and run by Sodexho – a French catering company founded in Marseilles in 1966. This is certainly here and now. This is the PFI Blair inheritance of Thatcher's attack on coal-fired stations.

Only in Dreamtime will be revoked the curse of barrenness laid on Agecroft Hall's Dauntsey Family for their apostasy from Catholicism. The PFI prison and its young offenders on substance abuse courses will all fly away; the cooling towers will topple elegantly upwards again; Agecroft Hall, or its replica in American Oak, will be shipped back from Virginia. **PP**

Prestwich: *An Asylum and a Hunting Park* - On the right, approaching Junction 17 from the West, is Philips Park in Prestwich. Part of its former West Wood now lies under the M60 on the left – if it had run a little further to the north the Motorway would have expensively clipped Whitefield Golf Course.

But Philips Park really is a park – probably a mediaeval deer park. The estate was acquired in 1799 by the same Philips family that provided Manchester with its first MP. A house was built called The Park – demolished in 1950. The stable block remains and is now a nightclub – once fashionable, because of its isolation, for rave events.

Nearby is Prestwich Hospital – in less politically correct times known as the County Lunatic Asylum. Erected in 1851 after the 1846 County Lunatic Asylums Act, it was originally brick with stone facings, and had space for 500 inmates with segregated blocks for male and female. By 1913 it had been extended to accommodate 1020 inmates.

Above: Three Arches. Part of the demolished Victorian Buildings at Prestwich 'County Lunatic Asylum'. The portico stands at the end of landscaped gardens surrounded by remaining low-rise Victorian buildings.

The Asylum was a self-contained world – chapel, farm, gardens, electrical power generation, bowling green – you might never need, or indeed want, to leave.

The modern patients have now been decanted into the community, but still live around the hospital. Land, with which the Victorians were so profligate, has been sold off for housing and a Tesco Supermarket. But there is still one surprise and haven of tranquility – a Healing Garden, laid out on geomantic principles. According to this lore, here a Dragon Line running west-east from the Irish to the North Sea intersect the City's Mind Line at a spring. The Mind Line runs south, gathering force, past the ancient refuge and ferry at Kersal Cell to St Mary's

Church, hidden away in the City's heart. It penetrates Manchester's Central Reference Library, both Universities, the Whitworth Art Gallery and finally, Platt Hall Gallery of Costume. Here, in a Maze, is the Mind of the Goddess.

On the other side of Junction 17 there is a piece of pure placename delight: 'Besses o' th' Barn.' It is unusual for the Ordnance Survey and General Post Office to have allowed any dialect to sully their nomenclature, (though Manchester also gets away with 'Irlam o' th' Heights' on the A6). Here the two naming authorities probably got it wrong: Bess is reputed to have been landlady of an inn with a barn attached – so it should be: 'Bessy's, o' th' Barn.' **PP**

Remembering: *Haweswater* - One of the reasons why the City of Manchester wanted to buy Heaton Park (see Junction 19) was to build a reservoir. It is the highest point in the City, so that water could flow to all parts by gravity. The reservoir took a long time to build: plans were made in 1904 as soon as the park was in city ownership and work started in 1907, but it was not completed until 1926.

Above: Lancashire County Lunatic Asylum at Prestwich Named in less politically correct times, this vast Victorian undertaking was a village in itself. Erected in 1851 it is now Prestwich Hospital next to Junction 17 at the head of the M60 Motorway.

The water to fill it travels eighty-two miles, taking thirty-six hours, from a lake even higher up - Haweswater in Lancashire – now Cumbria. Manchester had already been drinking, brewing and washing in water from Thirlmere since 1895, and Longdendale before that, but it was never enough.

The inflow of water into Heaton Park is controlled by a little valve station on the northern edge of the reservoir called the Terminal Building, which was built

in 1955 by the City Engineers. It fronts onto Heywood Road in Prestwich (which never gets to Heywood; it turns into a dirt track after Simister – See Junctions 18,19 & 20). The Haweswater scheme was a massive undertaking, but there was little visible to show for the expense, except the water in your tap, so the City commissioned a Work of Art. It is by Mitzi Cunliffe, an American who lived in England from 1949 to 1976, with much of her work carved or modelled in a small garage at her home in Didsbury in south Manchester.

A carving in relief on Lake District slate, typically 1950s in style, shows the whole thing in symbolic form. At the top is Haweswater, with a suggestion of the fells round about. Out of it comes the big pipe of the aqueduct. Part of it is buried, to indicate the cut-and-cover sections. In the middle, and dominating the composition, three men with heroically big hands and feet are sealing a joint with poured lead. At the bottom, pure water pours forth like fruit from a cornucopia. Underneath it, five more slate panels give the whole history of the undertaking, with all the dates and names and statistics.

Inside the valve house all is calm; the machinery is painted pale blue, there are sectional maps on the walls and 3-D models in glass cases. Through the windows overlooking the reservoir can be seen the outlet towers on the far side. It is like some hushed temple to period technology, or to the Goddess of Water. MH

Heaton Park: *Peoples Park or Stately Demesne* - Heaton Park, comprising 640 acres, was bought by Manchester Corporation in 1902 for £230,000 (still a bargain at £15mn in today's prices). Successive Earls of Wilton had been trying unsuccessfully to sell it for some time, notably in 1866 and again in 1896 when the whole estate was divided up on paper into building plots. The Earls of Wilton, also Egertons, had made the park into a stately private demesne from about 1805 onwards.

Left: Haweswater water at Heaton Park Reservoir: Mural by Mitzi Cunliffe at Heaton Park reservoir. The pump house is on Simister Road on the north side of the reservoir. The mural depicts engineers bringing water from Haweswater in the Lake District to Manchester.

The great perimeter wall, twelve feet high and reputedly five miles long, was built in 1807-14, and the gates and lodges at much the same time. Within the walls the old field boundary hedges and walls were cleared away and an English Park created with smooth rolling turf and carefully placed clumps and belts of trees, on the Capability Brown model although not, as it happens, by Capability Brown but by William Emes and John Webb.

It was a private paradise, but not if a public road ran through it, right past the mansion. So the old public roads were closed and new ones made outside the park's boundaries. That is why Sheepfoot Road and Middleton Road are so broad and straight. Old and untidy farms and cottages, together with the people who lived in them, had to go too. The people were re-housed out of sight in Simister or Rhodes, or in the lodges or the Home Farm.

The result was beautiful. There is nothing more pleasing to the eye than an English park of the great landscaping tradition, that art of shaping and planting on a grand scale to create a world that looks completely natural, like a piece of Eden before the fall. The art that is perhaps the greatest contribution England has made to all the arts. Especially when, as here, the landscape is naturally beautiful, rolling, high, and airy.

So the Egertons enjoyed their splendid solitude for the best part of a century, occasionally bringing the park to life when the Heaton Races were held, or a soirée filled the great mansion on the hill with music.

The bow windows at the front of the mansion looked out towards Manchester. In 1805 it was only a small busy town four miles away. Even as late as 1879 the Lancashire and Yorkshire Railway was forced into a tunnel under the Park by the opposition of the Earl. But by 1902 Manchester had become a great smoky metropolis lapping right up to the gates. Finally the sale of the ancestral land was agreed. Manchester needed a public park, a green lung where the people could escape from the rush and grime and toil. Manchester also needed clean water, in particular a holding reservoir on high ground for the water brought from Thirlmere and Haweswater in Westmorland.

What Manchester did not need, or did not think it needed, was a stately home. So the superb furniture and fitments of the mansion were speedily sold off and the house became an extra-grand tearoom. The Parks Department soon got to work on the Park. Drives and paths were widened and tarmacked, iron fencing was put up, pink cherries, yellow laburnums and orange Altrincham Maples were planted in quantity. Bowling greens were made in front of the mansion and a public golf course set out. A boating lake was dug, and in an unusual burst of serendipity the portico of the old Manchester Town Hall, just then being demolished in King Street, was re-erected as a truly stately foil to Heaton. It was essential that the new park should be accessible to all, so a tram line was brought in to a terminus by the boating lake. You could take a tram direct from the hurly-burly of Piccadilly to the sylvan calm of Heaton. The tram shed in the Park and the lines down to the gates are incidentally the only remaining piece of Manchester's original tram system. And the Lancashire and Yorkshire Railway is now part of the Manchester Metrolink light rail – the Papal Monument to the visit of John Paul II in 1982 is perched above its tunnel.

And so the people of Manchester have enjoyed their People's Park, one of the largest and finest Municipal Parks in the country, for a whole century. The children whose bums polished smooth the backs of the

Left: Heaton Hall and Park:.Heaton Hall has now undergone reconstruction, and the gardens have now been restored to how they would have looked when the hall and park were first built in the 18th century.

Above: Heaton Park Folly. Looking north west towards the telecommunications tower in Heaton Park from the bridge carrying Rochdale Road over the M60 motorway. Large electricity pylons follow the route of the motorway and River Irk.

Right: Manchester Old Town Hall on King Street in 1904. It was demolished in 1911 as dangerous. These Ionian columns now stand in Heaton Park.

King Street, Manchester.

bronze lions outside the mansion now pose their own grandchildren upon them.

But in the new Millennium, half of the great house is derelict, even if the rest has been painstakingly refurnished in the style of what the City so precipitately sold off in 1902. The Home Farm and the Dower House are abandoned, and so are the lodges. Carparking has got out of hand. Nearby is the giant telecommunications mast, which arrived as a not-altogether-welcome additional folly in the 1960s, and the Parks' Department eyesore of a tip.

Now Heritage Fund Lottery money is to hand, and work is under way, to return Heaton to its former glory. But which former glory? Stately Demesne or People's Park? **MH**

Heaton Park: *The Temple* - When Lord Wilton, the youthful builder of Heaton Hall, made his Grand Tour of Europe in 1784-5 he recorded his impressions in 'picturesque' language. The term was not a vague one. It meant seeing the real landscape as though it was a painted one, subject to the rules of artistic composition.

Not just any painting either; specifically, a painting by Claude or Poussin. On his second Tour of 1787-8 he bought two 'Claude Glasses' (for 8s-6d, or £35 today) with which to observe the landscape more poetically. You sat with your back to the view and observed its reflection, tinted, and framed. Claude's landscapes are adorned with temples, but they are gentle, Mediterranean – not much like Heaton. But in 1803 Wilton was touring nearer to home, in the Lake District. Ignored until then as a rude

wilderness, its beauties had been unlocked by a new appreciation of the Sublime, stronger stuff than the gentle Picturesque.

Now Wilton could see the capabilities of his hilly domain at Heaton, aided by William Emes in shaping the landscape, and by James or Samuel Wyatt who designed its crowning feature, The Temple. A plate of Heaton Park in Aiken's 'Forty Miles around Manchester' of 1793 shows the house,

then newly builded, but no temple. In 1807 'The Beauties of England and Wales' shows The Temple as well, 'which commands very extensive views into Yorkshire, Cheshire, Derbyshire and Staffordshire.' So we can date it pretty closely. And its location ensured that some two centuries later the Temple would itself be visible from the M60 Motorway – though perhaps to more hurried sensibilities.

The design of the Temple is a curious one. Its prototype is the famous Tempietto of Bramante in Rome, in turn based on ancient Roman temples: a circular drum with a ring of columns round it and a dome for a roof. Very elegant, it looks good from all directions, but has no known practical use (although Lord Wilton, in addition to his 'glasses,' did own a telescope). The curious thing about the Heaton Temple is that it has another, miniature, temple on the top. It is a fractal, like a classical pagoda. The hill it sits on is in turn shaped like a domed roof. Recently restored as part of the Heaton Park Restoration Masterplan (a grandiose title which would have pleased Lord Wilton, funded by Lottery money), it is to be a public summer studio for local artists (which at least approaches Claude's Glasses).

The Temple in its circular colonnaded form echoes the centre of the mansion, which is semicircular and temple-like. Both forms have found a match in a set of buildings on the opposite hilltop from a different era altogether. In Blackley Cemetery are the municipal Crematorium, with its semicircular bow, and the circular Temple of Remembrance. They were designed by the City architect, L.C. Howitt, in 1959. Although executed in rough concrete, and none too refined, they stand in just the same relation to each other and to the rolling landscape as the hall and temple across the valley. The 1950s and 60s were an age when architects seemed to take a perverse pleasure in ignoring the past and disregarding the genius of the place, so Mr Howitt deserves thanks for looking around and taking a hint from his distinguished predecessors. **MH**

Left: The Temple, Heaton Hall Park. The Temple was restored in 2000 to its former state, and is now protected by a metal fence. It stands on the highest point within the boundaries of the City of Manchester, and has views to the north and north east towards Oldham.

Distribution on the M60 - Regional and National distribution road centres are studded around the M60 – Sainsbury and Tesco (both at Middleton); Iceland and Boots (Rochdale and Heywood) and three for the Co-operative (Manchester, Gorton and Heywood).

These centres, which generate vast amounts of traffic, are the end result of much ingenuity and evolution, and represent considerable investment in inventory systems and handling techniques. Road haulage is the area where local and national government must tread carefully – where the Department of Transport floats ideas in 'Freight Quality Partnerships.' A wrong step here, and petrol vanishes from garages, food fails to arrive at supermarkets, Motorways are blocked by tractors and HGVs.

Since 1950 the number of lorries in Britain has fallen from about 600,000 to 420,000 currently. This is due in part to the introduction of juggernauts, but also to better logistics and such innovations as side-loaders. But recent projections in 2004 suggest that this is about to change. Lorries can get no larger, smart logistics improvements are slowing. Only more trucks can haul our consumer goods. The number of cars is up from 4 million to 23 million in the same period since 1950 and seems to have no upper limit.

Tesco is overall the largest distributor in the area with over 400,000 sq. ft. Its 'Slow Moving Goods' centre at Middleton is 165,000 sq. ft., and serves some 258 stores via the M60; its Temperature Controlled Distribution Centre is even more massive: 240,000 sq. ft. for some 59 stores. Boots comes next with its National Distribution Centre at Heywood, with some 255,000 sq. ft. Manchester also has 'generic centres': the Trafford Park Eurofreight Terminal, and the World Freight Terminal at Manchester Airport (the latter 550,000 sq. ft. handling 125,000 tonnes a year). But none of these can compete with their US cousins – Unilever has only five 'super warehouses' in the States, each of one million square feet.

Above: Trafford Centre Container Terminal. On the left, with ornate lamp posts, is the newly constructed slip road leading from the motorway into the Trafford Centre's huge car park. The dome of the centre rises up above the Harry Potter film billboard advert. Capture date is 31st May, 2004.

Above: Imperial War Museum
North: designed by Daniel
Libeskind, stands on Trafford
Wharf on the south bank of the
Manchester Ship Canal, next to
the Hovis Flour Mill. Here it is
reflected in calm waters of the
canal on the afternoon of
Christmas Day 2003.

Immediately outside the M60 area, Woolworths, Safeway, Somerfield and ASDA all have important distribution centres; the total square footage for the M60 catchment area is probably about 2.5 mn. feeding daily perhaps 4000 HGV loads onto the M60, with similar return journeys. With 'just in time' logistics, the average stay of goods in a distribution centre may be only 5 hours. This kind of industry, if it may be so called, creates its own jobs: HGV and forklift truck drivers, refrigeration maintenance engineers, and all the associated skills of IT managers, security guards, pallet suppliers – and logistics training.

In August 2003 Bolton, to the North of the M60, launched 'Logistics College North West', the UK's largest, providing 500 Modern Apprenticeships for the 'Young LGV Driver Scheme.' LGVs (Large Goods Vehicles) are at 7.5 tonnes+ heavier than HGVs of 3.5 tonnes+. New trained drivers are certainly needed. Much of Manchester's imported consumer goods, replacing Britain's hollowed out manufacturing base, will come via Hull and Liverpool docks – where 'intermodal freight villages' – trans-shipment of goods to lorries – are the buzz global village term.

And so-called 'rigid HGVs' over 7.5 tonnes have the highest accident rate in the UK, at 993 accidents for every billion kilometers – car accidents run at 853/bn km., though most of us struggle to hit 10,000 miles a year in the old Ford jamjar.

Kellogg's the cornflake people, who manufacture at Trafford Park, may stand for many of the aspects of globalised distribution: it is a US company that most people believe to be British. Although its products were only launched in the UK in the 1920s, they have effectively dislodged the 'full English breakfast.' The UK and Ireland are the largest per capita consumers of Kellogg's breakfast products in the world at about 6 kilos per person per year. Up the Manchester Ship Canal comes annually about 400,000 tonnes of maize for Cerestar to process. There are 108 varieties of

breakfast cereal in the average Tesco – all different, all needing to be stocked, many originating at the Trafford Park Kellogg's factory. Here the day shift is hardly a dozen workers, making a whole nation's laxative cornflakes or Special K, which is then boxed, palletised, shrink-wrapped and delivered in by computers to despatch bays for the waiting sideloaders, with no human intervention.

Kellogg's European manufacturing operations are run from Manchester. And not just manufacturing: from Manchester Kellogg's computer servers support the rest of the UK, Italy, Germany and Spain, as well as sales operations in Ireland, Italy, Belgium, Holland, Denmark, Finland, Norway, Sweden and France. This is a complex world of value added services that creates local jobs – taking up the slack of lost mills and mines.

Near to its Trafford Park manufacturing plant, Kellogg's is now building another new 35,000 sq. m. high-bay pallet store and distribution facility. This is a 14m high building, set on 17 acres to accommodate over 30,000 pallet positions. The development includes space for 137 cars and 106 lorries.

There is a cost to pay for all this efficiency: Lorries are a major source of air pollution in the Greater Manchester area – about one third of all nitrogen oxide and another third of fine particle pollution is from Lorries. Projections now suggest that much of Manchester within the M60 box will continue to exceed national air quality guidelines beyond 2005. Britain now has one of the highest asthma rates in the world – with an estimated 10 million sufferers. Good that the M60 Motorway system is there to deliver the drugs needed. **PP**

Alkrington Hall, Rhodes and Simister - Alkrington Park is one of Manchester's few surviving stately homes, and one with a surprising history. It contained both Alkrington Hall and Sir Ashton Lever's Museum of Curiosities. The hall, a big plain red-brick job, looking down over Rhodes, was built for Darcy Lever in 1735-7.

Its architect was Giacomo Leoni, Italian economic migrant and translator of Palladio and Alberti, who also designed the superb garden facade of Lyme Hall. Here in about 1760 Lever's son, Sir Ashton Lever, initiated a famous museum of natural history and curiosities. The story goes that he shot and preserved a white sparrow, which triggered the collecting bug. By 1773, when he was elected to the Royal Society, he was receiving as many as a thousand people in a day to view his collection. A visitor in 1774 described it as occupying 'four large rooms ranging almost the whole front of the building, the wall formerly dividing the apartments being formed into arches to support the chambers above.'

Today Alkrington Hall is subdivided to make four houses. Its park still sweeps down from the North front to the river Irk, framed by woods. But on the South, Alkrington Garden Village, begun in 1909, has swallowed up its estate, leaving a series of ponds and a formal canal mixed up with the houses. As for the famous collection, Sir Ashton over-reached himself and had to sell it all by lottery. Some specimens were bought by Lord Derby, and ended up in Liverpool Museum.

Rhodes

Alkrington Hall looks down from its aristocratic height on the village of Rhodes. Definitely a village, despite its proximity to Middleton and Manchester.

Lancashire is a great mixture of valleys and hills, industry, stately homes, working-class housing, and motorways, but it is not often you can see all of them together, as here. The series of reservoirs by the Irk belonged to Salis Schwabe & Co.'s great calico printing works, which had one of the tallest chimneys in the world. The Schwabes lived in the plain Rhodes House of 1811, now the Golf Clubhouse.

Among the brick terraces and 1930s improved housing are several early works by one of Manchester's most distinguished architects, who mixed Arts-and-Crafts with Art Nouveau: Edgar Wood. They are: Rhodes School of 1884, now Woods Court; and a couple of groups of houses: 31 to 37 Broad Street (1899), and 2 to 4 Schwabe Street (1895).

Simister

Virtually on top of junction 18, the northernmost point of the M60, but inaccessible from it, is the village of Simister. The east side of the M60 leads onto the M66 towards Bury, the west side onto the

trans-Pennine M62, and it is all cobbled together by means of a motorway roundabout. Great roads lead in all directions, but, aloof from it all, Simister is connected to the outside world only by a couple of dirt tracks at one end and a single tarmac road into Prestwich at the other.

The village is a single straggling street, with a little church of 1915 called St George's and a pub called the Same Yet. Why the Same Yet? Because the sign painter took too literally his instructions to paint the new sign 'the same yet,' when it should have been the same as the old one. The school, now the village hall, was provided by Lady Wilton of Heaton Hall in about 1850. The little church, a chapel-of-ease to St Margaret's in Prestwich and designed by R.B. Preston, was finished in 1915.

Isolated and severed, yet seeming to rejoice in these qualities, Simister seems inward looking, hardly noticing the low ground below and the higher ground of Lancashire away to the north. MH

Above: Simister Church. The church stands just off the main street of the village which is separated from nearby Heaton Park and Prestwich by the M60 Motorway at Junction 16.

Birds on the M60: *Migrants, Vagrants & Asylum Seekers* - The M60 Motorway cuts across a wide range of bird habitats, but its construction, although passing through some rural areas, has not had an entirely negative effect on birdlife. The M60 area in fact runs from rural to urban, lowland to peak, across rivers, lake and wetlands.

There are also surprisingly large stands of woodland, for example at Botany Bay Wood near Chat Moss (Junction 12).

All these areas provide habitats for birds. Over 300 species have been recorded locally – though only about 200 appear in any year: one dedicated Greater Manchester watcher has managed 176 species in a year – the record so far. Manchester has in fact been well served since at least the 1800s by careful observation of its birdlife – summer migrants were catalogued in 1822 by Blackwall who noted the first to arrive as the Sandmartin (April 6th) and the last as the shy Nightjar (May 19th) which unfortunately no longer breeds in the district.

The M60 area also harbours nationally important numbers of wintering birds: Pochard and Tufted Duck roosting on Chorlton Water Park (Junction 5) in the daytime, feeding on Salford Quays at night; and 100+ Goldeneye roosting at night on Heaton Park Reservoir (Junction 17) while feeding on the River Irwell during the day.

The M60 area is speckled with the reservoirs of thirsty Manchester. Audenshaw Reservoir to the East (between Junctions 23 and 24) is in fact three beds and is a major halt for many birds. No. 3 bed was drained during the construction of the M60, but re-filled after the Motorway was completed. It is slightly smaller than before but the new, gently sloping, sand-coloured stone edges have provided attractive feeding areas for visiting waders. Audenshaw remains a prime location for sighting many birds, with 208 recorded species, and significant numbers of Goldeneye, Golden and Grey Plover, Lapwing, Pochard, Tufted Duck, Canada Goose, Great Crested Grebe and occasionally such rarities as Widgeon, Hobby, Peregrine Falcon, Turnstone, Mediterranean Gull, Purple Sandpiper and Rock Pipits.

Black-Headed Gulls are another bird present at Audenshaw, but in vast numbers – in excess of 6,500 were seen in December 2002, drawn by pickings on the municipal tips; the use of rubbish tips by gulls is a relatively recent change in behaviour. Curious to note, therefore, that in 1860 this Gull was a rarity here and a singleton visitor was, in true Victorian manner, immediately shot dead at Withington. These modern flocks are both resident (a local breeding population) and incomers – many from Estonia and Latvia.

The three bodies of water to the West of the M60 at Chorlton (Junction 5), Sale (between Junctions 6 and 7) and the hidden, mysterious and inaccessible Loonts Lake (Junction 4), are all "borrow pits" – lakes formed by extracting gravel for the M60 motorway construction, or else dead of arms of the diverted River Mersey. These adventitious lakes have been of definite benefit to birds in the County, particularly waterfowl.

Kestrels hovering over the M60's verges have benefited by the vibration of the traffic which is believed to bring out voles and other edible items, onto which they pounce vertically. On the negative side, Barn Owls tend to fly into vehicles when hunting along the M60's grassy margins. To the north, in the Irwell valley, (Junction 19) confused Swans land on the M60 not infrequently, there being water on either side of the Motorway at that point. It has also been demonstrated that songbirds are

adversely affected by Motorway noise: they cannot hear each other, and so cannot establish breeding territories. The one bird, however, that can give motorists a literal run for their money is the Swift, capable of reaching 110 km per hour (approaching 70 mph), and one of the few to be able to overtake you at legal M60 motoring speeds.

Birding on the M60 is not entirely inappropriate, given that the Royal Society for the Protection of Birds began in Didsbury (Junction 3) in 1889, where, with typical Didsbury high-mindedness, it pledged to put down the millinery craze for wearing the plumage of rare birds in hats, particularly that of Egrets. It was therefore with some pleasure that the Greater Manchester County Recorder for Birds was able in 2002 to report a Great White Egret, more common in the Balkans and Black Sea, was at both Sale and Chorlton Water Parks (between Junctions 6 and 7). Although it has only ever been seen about 100 times in Britain, it has since reappeared in the Greater Manchester area in May 2004.

Mute Swans are perhaps the most easily identified local birds. They mate for life and females may be fertile for two decades or more. It seems therefore a particular sacrilege that in 2002 a pair was actually shot dead on their nest in Ashton-under-Lyne. Local reports show that Swans are subjected to the usual indignities: dying from eating discarded fish hooks and lead weights, robbed of their eggs, polluted with oil, and shot at with airguns. Yet not all gloom – a 1982 Manchester survey predicted impending extinction, but at present around 80-90 pairs attempt breeding annually. Of these, 60-70 produce cygnets. The total Greater Manchester County population of these splendid creatures is probably around 500.

Equally identifiable now, but perhaps less welcome, is the invasive Canada Goose, with its black and white head, mottled plumage and hungry habits.

There are well over 2500 in the area, and their eggs are regularly pricked out under official government licence to control the population. Large numbers are visible on Audenshaw reservoir from September onwards, with significant resident populations at Sale Water Park (150) and Chorlton (60). This bird was introduced into Britain in the 17th century, and was until recently relatively rare – in 1982 there were only 10 breeding pairs locally.

At times the numbers of birds congregating within sight of the M60 can be vast – in 2002 Starlings were present in a huge whirling group of 10,000+ on Carrington Moss (Junction 8). A group of 2500 Jackdaws was also seen in the same area, yet many

Mancunians would be hard pressed to identify this bird, once a common chimney nuisance in the City centre.

As with its vibrant street characters, Greater Manch-ester also has its bird oddities. Sightings include a North American Bald Eagle called Sydney, an African Grey Parrot, a Chinese Golden Pheasant, a pink Greater Flamingo and two Australian Black Swans. Discretion draws a veil over activities of the South American Nanday Conure (a bright yellow and red parrot) imaginatively described as forming a ménage à trois with two local black and white Magpies.

The Owl House At Abney Hall (Junction 4)

There appear to be only two Owl Houses in Britain; one is in Norfolk, and the other is at Abney Hall (see Junction 4). This is an elegant octagonal Gothic tower with a conical roof, and it stands on the corner of the old walled garden, now filled with offices and car parking, not a stone's throw from the M60. The idea was, presumably, to encourage nesting owls, who would feed their young on pestiferous mice. It was probably built as part of Travis & Magnell's make-over of Abney Hall in the 1850s for James Watts.

....and The Dovecote at Sale Hall (Junction 6)

In the 1840s and 50s Walter and Mary Worthington rebuilt Sale Old Hall. As part of the work they commissioned a distinguished Manchester architect and distant relation, Thomas Worthington, to build them a new dovecote. It was octagonal below, circular above, with a somewhat Scottish-looking conical roof with big dormers. The doves were probably ornamental, though historically pigeons have been kept as a tasty winter snack, the Lord's birds fattened on the pillaged fields of his peasant neighbours. Former working dovecotes are still standing at Tatton Park farm, at Alderley Park (now Astra-Zeneca and grandly called a Columbarium), and at Jodrell Hall (now Terra Nova School).

When the Old Hall was demolished in the 1920s the dovecote survived, only to be partly engulfed by the embankment of the M60 Motorway at Junction 6. Now the M60 has been widened, and the dovecote moved to a new home at Walkden Gardens. But pieces of the fine blue and doubtless expensive Lakeland roof slates can still be found in the spoilheaps. One wonders if a hunting night owl might fly here from Abney Hall, in search of a roosting dove. Four miles there and four miles back, in the darkness. A Lord Mayor's predatory owls beat doves in a dovecote any day – even if both buildings are only mock gothic. **PP**

Chadderton Cotton Mills & a Fake Pub - Oldham is a hilltop town; that much is obvious from the motorway, especially since the Borough Council built a lumpish office block, Oldham Civic Centre, right on the summit. It has no river to speak of, for either water power or transport. Indeed it has no visible natural resources at all.

All the more astonishing therefore that, of all the cotton towns of Lancashire, Oldham was the most prodigious. It was the one that grew the quickest, from most insignificant beginnings. By the 1880s it was the cotton spinning capital of the world. And, when the fall finally came, it was the town that crashed the hardest.

Typical Oldham mills are high and wide and foursquare, generously windowed, shiny and redbrick. ACE, GORSE, RAM, and RUGBY, they proclaim their names in white glazed brick on their corner towers. A little further is RAVEN, accompanied by an impressive forest of mill chimneys. But during the First World War ACE

MILL was diverted for use as Oldham Aircraft Factory. Soon after completion in 1914 it was adapted and expanded for the assembly of Handley Page 0/400 heavy bombers. Maintenance and assembly sheds, stores, offices, etc. survive on site. They are utilitarian sheds, some with Belfast roofs and some with lightweight iron roofs. High and dry, the buildings are still in government use, being part of HMSO, no doubt stockpiling reports of the Highway Agency on Britain's Motorways.

They are an incredibly localised assemblage: they all date from the early years of the twentieth century; in fact RAVEN, RUGBY, RAM, and GORSE were built one after the other in only two years, and all except

eft: The Owl Tower at Abney
all, probably erected in
e 1850s for a Lord Mayor
Manchester.

Above: Chadderton Mill
One of several mills in
Chadderton, each one with
characteristic design of tower
with white letters. A former
waste pond is now used by
anglers. The scene is overgrow
but the mills are still in use,
providing space for light
industry and are well-maintaine

Above: Gorse Mill

Gorse Mill, Chadderton, another
of many mills around Oldham
and Manchester, with the name
of the founding company in
large white letters. Neo-classical
columns adorn the red brick
tower. The building appears to
have been recently renovated
with new roof tiles and clean
brickwork.

RUGBY were built by the Stotts – a dynasty of mill architects. These were all state-of-the-art industrial units, concrete and steel framed, blazing with electric light at night, powered by steam engines that were things of beauty; and they all operated ranks of locally Oldham-manufactured spinning machinery. All this, at a time when Lancashire and Britain led the world in cotton.

The export of looms down the Manchester Ship Canal to India and China, the advent of man-made fibres, two world wars and the Great Depression eventually sapped strength and initiative. The departure of Directors from Manchester's grimy centre for salubrious addresses in Cheshire (as early as the 1850s) did not make help to make for social cohesion. In 1882-84 Britain had over 80% of the world's cotton trade. Even at the onset of the Great Depression in 1929, it had 60 million spindles out of the world total of 164 million, and a quarter of the world's 3 million looms. It was estimated that 10 million Britons owed their jobs to King Cotton. By 1939 it had only 28% of the world cotton textile trade, though of a bigger pie. By 1958, for the first time in the long history of its textile trade, Britain imported more cotton good than it exported. The Cotton Exchange in Manchester (now a theatre) lingered for another decade; the last 1968 price quotation for Egyptian Staple is still visible on its display boards inside.

Of course Manchester bounced back. A quarter of the UK's population did not emigrate (as one commentator prophesied) when cotton collapsed. Service industries, tourism and the heritage industry took up some of the slack. Just look, for example, at the Boat and Horses Inn.

In between the mills are the red-brick terraces where the mill workers lived, and the pubs where they spent their money. One was the Boat and Horses. The M60 destroyed it, and blocked up the canal that gave it its name. The new Boat and Horses is a very

curious concept pub, because it is themed to look like an old industrial building - but emphatically not like the real industry that is all around. This is the friendly face of industry. Where the real mills were all hard red brick, grid windows, flat roofs and rectilinearity, this is higgledy-piggledy, low-rise, hand-made, with cosy slate roofs and nice sign-painting. In front is the recreated canal. The pub is off-the-peg, all new, but looks old, and it is a roaring success. **MH**

Above: A fake pub - The Boat and Horses

Three Lost Utopias at Junction 23 - There is still a strong streak of non-conformist religion in Manchester and its surrounding towns and cities. Perhaps the interests of Lancashire cloth makers were always opposed to those of farmer and landowner: Manchester was Republican in the Civil War, Stuart Royalist in the 1745 Jacobite rebellion, and against the landowners during the Corn Law agitation of the 1830s.

It is not therefore surprising that it has harboured a long line of religious and political visionaries who either sprang from, or fed into this radicalism.

But no movement was perhaps stranger than the Messianism of John Wroe, who expected the New Jerusalem to be built in the prosperous market town of Ashton-Under-Lyne. It has inspired a novel and a television series (Mr Wroe's Virgins). The documents which might reveal the whole truth have long been suppressed. There are also no known photographs or paintings of Wroe – perhaps his ugliness reinforced

his view that graven images were sinful. The bare bones are clear. Born in Bradford in 1782, Wroe crossed the Pennines in 1820, and found in Ashton-under-Lyne a fertile seedbed for his increasingly odd religious views. Physically repulsive, dishevelled, with an unkempt beard and speaking broad Yorkshire dialect, he must have possessed some gift to overcome these impediments – charisma, but not in our modern vacuous celeb style. He seems to have been a ferocious preacher; he attempted unsuccessfully to walk across the River Tame where it divides Lancashire from Cheshire, (a drenching

reported by the devout as his baptism); he was publicly circumcised; he requested and was given seven virgin brides by his congregation. He chastised the ungodly, particularly women, with the birch below the pulpit of his Sanctuary. And he had a vision – Ashton-Under-Lyne as the New Jerusalem. It was to be the City surrounded by a wall, a hortus conclusus, to be entered only by four commanding gates. The new Messiah – or Shiloh was to be born here. Wroe, now called the Prophet, had become an Old Testament patriarch, extreme even by Victorian standards.

Given these illuminations, it is perhaps curious that Wroe has left no monument in Ashton, which is otherwise full of interesting buildings: his church, The Sanctuary, was partly wrecked by an angry mob who believed that Wroe, in an attempt to usher in the messiah, had been too intimate with a girl of twelve (disappointingly for Wroe and his movement, she bore him a girl). The Sanctuary, now demolished, was successively The Star theatre and cinema – a cruel and immoral fate for a prophet's tabernacle. His printing press, dedicated to producing the tracts of his Christian Israelite Church, was also demolished in the 1980s. Of the four square gatehouses with which his New Jerusalem was to be guarded, the Odd Whim public house is the sole survivor (again a cruel perversion of Wroe's vision of Albion). On inspection this building is usually swiftly dismissed as of no architectural merit or pedigree.

What does remain is the low square block of Melbourne house - the mansion which Wroe had built for himself for some £9000. But Melbourne House is away at Wakefield, back in Yorkshire: Wroe, accused of immorality with his young Ashtonian women, was obliged to leave Ashton, casting the dust of his New Jerusalem forever from his sandals as he plodded back over the Pennines. Australia, at the height of the gold rush, called to him; in 1853 Wroe answered, and new Christian Israelites in Melbourne provided the cash (or perhaps gold dust)

Right: Cradle for a Messiah
Cradle prepared for the birth of
Shiloh, the new Messiah, in the
New Jerusalem of Ashton-under-
Lyne by the British Israelites in
the1830s. The complete opposite
of the Founder's cattle trough or
manger, it was described as a
"beautiful little ark of blue silk
and gold" and said to have cost
£200, or four times a workman's
annual wage. It is now with
Joanna Southcott's Panacea
Society in Bedford.

and the name for his next English temple. He returned to England, to build and dedicate Melbourne House, said, incongruously to be modelled on Melbourne Town Hall. It had four gatehouses into its park. Perhaps the name was too prophetic: Wroe slipped and fell at antipodean Melbourne on a further visit in 1863, and breathed his last there, aged 82. His church and followers live on, down under, in warmer climes.

The Moravian Settlement at Fairfield

Nothing could be further, architecturally and spiritually, from the apocalyptic visions of John Wroe for Ashton-Under-Lyne than the quietist Moravian settlement at Fairfield: a church and a small group of 18th century houses that would not be out of place in New England.

The Moravian Settlement is just what it says: the onetime home of a group of settlers from Moravia (modern Czech Republic) who in 1785 came to Fairfield near Droylsden – just on the opposite side of Junction 23 from Ashton. But the peaceful Moravians long had their spiritual roots in Britain: they were founded in the 1450s by John Hus, who drank deep at the well of English religious reformer John Wycliffe. The Moravians, much harassed for their early Protestantism, wandered Europe for several centuries before they came to Manchester and prospered.

The Moravians have two lasting monuments: the fine collection of Georgian buildings at the Settlement, and Audenshaw Reservoir (now partly under the M60), designed by an illustrious Moravian: John Frederick LaTrobe Bateman – responsible for 10 reservoirs in all in the Manchester area, following the 1847 Manchester Corporation Waterworks Act.

In 1848 he began a chain of reservoirs near Glossop, supplying water to Manchester from the Pennine Hills. His five principal reservoirs in Longdendale Valley were then the largest reservoirs in the world

and Europe's first major water conservation scheme. The works were not finished for thirty years, until the spring rains of 1877. The reservoirs in the hills surrounding Tameside have never run dry – surely an appropriate metaphor for real religious inspiration.

Another Moravian architect relative, Benjamin LaTrobe, was even more successful – he was in part responsible for designing the White House in Washington - twice - his first attempt was burnt down by the British in 1811, and also for Baltimore's Catholic Cathedral.

And by some strange underground synchronism, the Governor of Victoria when gold digger John Wroe first set foot in Melbourne in 1853 was Moravian Charles Joseph LaTrobe. Much loved, he had to cope within the space of four short months with his own apocalypses as Governor: the destruction of Melbourne by drought and fire, and the discovery of the devil's metal, gold.

The Monastery of St Francis at Gorton

Ashton-under-Lyne shows how a promised Utopia can vanish utterly from sight. The Fairfield Moravian Settlement survives, sub-let and genteel. But the Monastery of St Francis at Gorton, founded by Franciscan Friars in 1863, has had a far more caustic solution poured over it – urban improvement. Here the Franciscans scrounged and laboured to throw up a statement: here they ministered to the poor of Manchester, daily celebrating beauty among poverty for nearly a century.

How then did this extraordinary building become so dilapidated, neglected and vandalised? This strange piece of Victorian Gothic is, after all, by Edward and Peter Paul Pugin, sons of the famous Pugin of Houses of Parliament fame (and also of Abney Hall at Junction 2). It is 'a triumph of Catholic Architecture' complete with rose windows, all in red and blue brick, with slate roofs. The interior is a frozen tribute

Top: Gorton Monastery. An Angel for Adoption.
Angel and Gospel on the wall of the Monastery of Gorton. This was captured on the Heritage Open Day September 1999. After the church was vacated in 1985, much of the interior was stolen or vandalised. It is currently being restored, and the Angels can be adopted for £50. It is close to Junction 23

Above: Gorton Monastery. The church of St Francis, Gorton Monastery, as it looked in September 1999 during the Heritage Open Day.

to post-1829 emancipation Catho-licism. Or, in the language of the Heritage Lottery Fund restoration bid applicant, it is Grade II* listed.

The answer is course planners' blight: in the 1960s the communities and congregations which had supported the Monastery for a century were broken up and rehoused from their back-to-backs. Local support and funding dwindled. The Monastery began to age, and had to be partly demolished in the 1970s. In 1989, the last Mass said, the brothers departed, and the property was sold for a development into apartments which never materialised. Vandalism increased, fixtures turned up in London auction rooms.

Now the developers have moved back. At the top of the funding pile are of course the new purse holders: the Heritage Lottery Fund, English Heritage and the European Fund. The abandoned Monastery is now to be 'a sacred space' and conference centre. Francis of Assisi might have smiled wryly at all this: 'the Pauper' was his chosen nickname; Poverty was his chosen mistress. In his youth he wandered penniless down through Moorish Spain into North Africa, among the disinherited Muslim Sufi brethren whom he later so much resembled. He knew that once the heart has ceased to beat, the Spirit blows where it wills and cannot be constrained, even by quangos. **PP**

Daisy Nook - The area known as Daisy Nook has always been a secluded spot, tucked away between Failsworth and Ashton, next to the meandering River Medlock. Despite the proximity of mills and factories, the nearby village of Woodhouses managed to preserve the lifestyle and accent of a bygone age well into the 20th century.

Today the M60 motorway sweeps across the River Medlock by Daisy Nook Garden Centre, but still the area is effectively off the beaten track, as there are no nearby junctions. The nearest exits are Ashton Junction 23 to the south and Failsworth Junction 22 to the north. Motorway drivers pass by Daisy Nook in a flash mostly unaware of the singular history and attractions of the area.

The name Daisy Nook only came into use in the latter part of the 19th century. Why was this? There is a

story, recounted in the Manchester City News of 1904 of how Charles Potter, the artist, was commissioned by celebrated dialect writer Mr Ben Brierley to go and make him a vignette drawing of the place portrayed as 'Daisy Nook' in his story 'A Day Out'. When the artist asked Brierley where it was situated, his response was 'I'veno particular place, theaw can fix it where theaw likes'. Potter went to Waterhouses, which he thought had been the inspiration for the story, and drew it. Following the success of this and other books by Ben Brierley, the area became popular with daytrippers and

soon everyone referred to it as 'Daisy Nook'.

Daisy Nook was depicted by LS Lowry. His painting 'Crime Lake' (1942) shows a lake full of rowing boats. Lowry includes a man apparently being arrested by two others after an unspecified incident, a visual pun on the name, which probably comes from the Crime family who once owned the estate.

It is not absolutely certain how Crime Lake came into being. According to one report it was deliberately flooded to provide water for the Fairbottam branch of the Ashton Canal. Another says flooding happened by accident following the collapse of one of the canal banks. There are rumours that a church was submerged beneath the lake and that you can hear its bells when the wind blows across the water, but it's more likely that only a couple of cottages were flooded.

In what is now known as Daisy Nook Country Park there are the remains of an industrial complex which has long since been overtaken by grass and weeds. The Hollinwood Branch canal had fallen into disuse by 1930. In 1938 the National Trust acquired 15 and a half acres of land there, and subsequently bought more. Up till the 1980s this was a derelict area and there were problems of pollution and foul smells. Thanks to regeneration money and the work of the

Greater Manchester Council, environmental improvements were carried out, paths and bridleways were laid, and much planting was undertaken.

A campaign group would like to restore the Hollinwood Branch canal. A new link would need to be constructed to take the canal across the motorway, now the only physical barrier which stands in its way. A restored canal would bring the park into greater, attracting lots more visitors. Daisy Nook is today still a place where people stroll, walk the dog, ride horses or engage in the quiet sport of angling. Cut off from the canal network, it retains its air of peace and seclusion. Perhaps that's one of its attractions and some would prefer it to stay that way. Heavy traffic passes along the M60 just beyond the trees, but as you stand and look out over Crime Lake, the modern world seems a very long way away. **AOR**

Left Crime Lake, Daisy Nook
View across Crime Lake taken
in December 1997. Once used
by boaters and a paddle
steamer, the waters of Crime
lake are now mostly still.
The lake, close to Junction 24,
is popular with anglers.

Denton Golf Course and Nico Ditch. There have been many ways for Mancunians, Lancastrians and Cestrians to impose their will on their differing landscapes: slash and burn, deforestation, Roman roads, hunting parks, opencast mining, canals, railways, motorways. But an enigmatic feature always attracts, and its sheer oddity may preserve it from erasure. Nico Ditch falls into this latter category.

No-one knows quite who or what Nico was, though since the Ditch dates from perhaps the AD 900s, it was certainly not Nico of The Velvet Underground, who whiled away some time in Prestwich. But if Prestwich is the head, Junction 7 the navel, then the Nico Ditch, which strikes the M60 at three o'clock at Denton Golf Course is the Godess's outstretched left arm – holding an SSI 6 golfing iron.

The Nico Ditch was about 5 miles long and where visible, four to five feet deep, as at Platt Fields Park in Fallowfield, Melland Playing Fields and on Denton Golf Course next to Junction 24 of the Motorway. Here the Nico Ditch has achieved true immortality by lending its name to Hole No.12, par 4, length 352 yards. Elsewhere it is invisible as a feature – passing unnoticed through Levenshulme via Matthews Lane, though other boundaries follow its lead – here the parish boundary between Levenshulme and Gorton.

The Nico Ditch is reputed to be an Anglo-Saxon or alternatively a Danish defensive earthwork, and has attracted vivid legends and folk etymologies: that the local Saxons were instructed to dig a section of the ditch each up to his own height to protect the

town of Manchester from invading Danes; that the ditch was constructed in a single night; that Manchester was ransacked after a bloody battle at the Ditch; that Reddish is Red Ditch (from the blood in Nico Ditch); Gorton is Gore Town (yet more blood) and Dane Bank (or Dane's Head Bank) refers to where the Danish Leader was slain; while 'Winning Hill' in Gorton refers to the outcome. All of this is memorable; none ascertainable; probably none true. The Nico Ditch has also nearly achieved the impossible, folklore status, but scoring almost zero internet hits.

Denton, on the Ditch, did not choose wisely in the industrial revolution: it specialised in the production of felt for hats, half sizes for men's hats (the Tweens), and mantles for gas lamps, all products with almost no conceivable modern market. Of the few bombs which fell here during the 1940 Manchester Blitz (which wreaked such havoc on Manchester City centre) one even-handedly also took out the Denton Golf Course Clubhouse. Its post-war replacement can be seen on the west side of Junction 24. Perversely, hats are not allowed to be worn inside... **PP**

Above: View of the Nico Ditch at Denton Golf Course. Nico Ditch has a rich local folklore, and is visible at several points in its five mile course. Here is runs over the Golf Course and its declivity, leading to a marshy sump, is a trap for the unwary. The M60 Motorway embankment is visible in the distance. Junction 24 and Audenshaw reservoir are not far away.

Nearly Every Junction: *Golf Courses & Clubhouses* - No spoilt walk around the M60 would be complete without a tally of the golf courses, since it is widely acknowledged that, just as the M25 links London's lunatic asylums, the M60 Motorway was built to provide access to Manchester's golf courses. There are at least 20 golf courses or golf driving facilities in and around the M60 Motorway (there are 2500 in the UK as a whole.)

This is not quite one at every junction of the M60, but time enough: new ones are constantly springing up. Junction 5 has Didsbury, from the 1890s, one of the oldest; others are at Withington, Northenden; then Sale and Chorlton-cum-Hardy (Jcn. 6); Ashton-on-Mersey (Jcn. 8) , Davyhulme (Jcn. 10), Boysnope (Junction 11), Worsley (Jcn. 13), Ellesmere (Jcn. 14), Kearsley (Jcn. 15) , Whitefield (Jcn. 17), North Manchester and Heaton Park (Jcn. 19), Blackley (Jcn. 20), Werneth (Jcn. 22), Fairfield and Denton (Jcn. 24), and at a stretch, Reddish Vale (Jcn. 27).

There have also been at least two golf courses

established by Manchester's prosperous but excluded Jewish communities – at Whitefield (est. 1932) in the north, and at Dunham Forest in the south. It will be interesting to see if golf will percolate to Manchester's many new immigrant communities – a Chinese Golf Course could be quite exotic, given the architectural extravagance of the Wing Yip supermarket on Oldham Road in Manchester, green animal ridge tiles and illuminated red plastic palm trees.

Between Junctions 9 and 10, next to the Trafford Centre, and on 61 hectares of Peel Holdings land there is also The Playgolf Experience, 'a £3.5 mn state of the art golf driving range' consisting of 64 bays on two levels. There is also a JJB store selling an 'unrivalled' range of golfing equipment and equipment, as well as a golfing academy. Golf is big. Its footprint on the landscape per head of user is vast. Its users are, definitionally, aspirant.

Didsbury Golf Course, one of the oldest, is famously split in two by the M60, with an expensive footbridge between the holes (look out for trolleys passing overhead between Junctions 5 and 6). The name is itself an anomaly, since the golf course does not lie in Didsbury, but in an ox-bow on the other side of the Mersey. The building of Simon's Bridge over the River Mersey in the 1890s allowed the Didsburghers to buy land for a nine hole course, now 18, par 70, at 6262 yards.

Pike Fold Golf Club, now near Bury, had to be removed completely from near Junction 20 during the construction of the M60. Not cheap. Apart from compensation (presumably paid by the motoring taxpayer to the golfplayer) the flit involved, according to the lawyers 'land acquisition, planning approval in the Green Belt, the design and construction of a new club-house and assistance to the golf course architect in the planning and construction of the course itself... a highly successful scheme.' At another affected course, the M60 motorway roar has been excluded by the erection of a 5 metre high, half mile long acoustic screen. Hardly on a par with the levelling of many local communities and houses, and their noise pollution.

The economics of golf are curious: you can buy a golf course for between £2 to £4mn. Or you can build your own: in the flush 90s some new schemes were coming in at a cost of £4mn, though an 18 hole course could be run up for about £500,000. Income from memberships and green fees is about £750,000, but maintenance and land rental can eat up half of that

in a year. So, your money back in 5 to 10 years. Sell up, move on. OK, but not stunning.

It is a pleasant and innocuous fancy to wonder what future generations of archaeologists in the year 4004 will make of these vast expanses of expensively designed, landscaped and maintained greens, mounds and sandy bunkers, all connected by the M60 – evidence of their real use being very small holes and little lost white balls.

The average Manchester 18-hole course requires some 90-150 acres, and will have about 100 players a day. All this conspicuous consumption of land and water at a time when the world population approaches six billion. Probably golf courses will in the future be as incomprehensible, technically and socially, as Silbury Mound and Stonehenge are to us, and open to as many mis-interpretations. St Andrew, presumably the patron saint of cross golfers, has much to answer for.

Perhaps the real anti-hero of golf courses is Mark Philips, provider of municipal parks and Member of Parliament for Manchester from 1833 to 1847. He had the foresight to put a penny on the rates and £1000 of his own money (£60,000 today) into the provision of municipal parks in Manchester – Philips Park in Manchester's Bradford area (opened 1846) is his monument. Other parks followed – Peel Park in Salford, Queens Park in Harpurhey, Boggart Hole Clough (1890), then Wythenshawe and Platt Fields. It would be impossible to contemplate such benevolent acts today – the cost of the land alone would be ruinous. Heaton Park (taken over by the City in 1902), is not only a people's park. Rather cheekily and perhaps aping its betters, it had to have a people's golf course - with a rather good pavilion shaped like a pie with one slice missing... **MH & PP**

The Fate of Old Halls in Cheshire and Lancashire - In the middle of the Mersey Bridge at Cheadle (Junction 3) is a stone engraved with a line between the initials L and C. So that is clear enough: Lancashire this side, Cheshire that. But on the east side of Stockport, where the Tame and the Goyt wind down to their confluence at the back of ASDA, it is very difficult to know which historic county you are in.

Lancashire or Cheshire? Derbyshire, or even Yorkshire? Hard to tell. Yet important. The fate of Lancashire and Cheshire Halls along the line of the M60 is instructive: few have survived unscathed the effects of two world wars and death duties: in the south the likes of Dunham Massey, Tatton and Tabley have joined the heritage industry, generally under the banner of the National Trust. Alderley Park now houses the Astra Zeneca Toxicology Unit. Abney Hall is offices. Sale Old Hall became too dangerous and was demolished. Marple Hall was allowed to fall down by its final heir, the writer Christopher Isherwood. Agecroft was dismantled and shipped to Virginia in 1925 – it can be visited on the internet. Heaton Hall was bought for the people by Manchester Corporation. The most melancholy of all is Stayley Hall at Stalybridge, which has been falling down seemingly forever, but hasn't quite managed to do so yet. One curiosity is Bradford Old Hall – you will find it on no maps: it had vanished by 1800, and so never appeared on any modern surveys. Excavation for the Commonwealth Games in East Manchester allowed archaeologists to locate the moat, timber and stone from the original 14th century dwelling. Resurrection, of a sort.

In its eastern stretches (Junctions 22 to 1) the M60 rises and falls as it cuts across a series of Pennine river valleys – the Medlock, the Tame, the Goyt. Where the Tame wiggles down into Reddish Vale, and the Goyt cuts round the back of Stockport, we find the best surviving group of old halls.

Arden, Arderne, or Harden Hall stands romantic and semi-ruined overlooking the Tame, and now the M60, near Junction 25. Its address is Battle Lane, Castle Hill, and it has a moat. It is built of stone, with crowstepped gables and a tall watchtower at the back. Big mullioned windows fill the remaining walls. A ruinous stone barn is nearby. Arden Hall was built in 1597 (date formerly on the right hand gable) for Ralph and Ellen Arderne. The Cheshire Ardernes (yes, we are in Cheshire) had a manor here in Bredbury, and another at Alvanley in Delamere forest, where there

is another Arderne Hall. Is there a relationship with the forest of Arden and the Warwickshire Ardens, the family of Shakespeare's mother? It would be nice to think so: Shakespeare is supposed to have spent time as a tutor in Catholic Lancashire in the dangerous invasion years of the 1580s, but there is little direct evidence of north country dialect, or Catholicism, in his plays.

Architecturally speaking the house shows us the Renaissance making its belated appearance in Cheshire, because unlike a medieval house it is symmetrical. At least it looks symmetrical. The front door is in the middle, but it opens at the side of the porch into a hall set asymmetrically on the right. The stair was straight ahead in the tower. So they had the best of both worlds, the old medieval hall with its high and low end and screens passage on

the inside, and the new-fangled symmetry on the outside. It was a wonderfully dusty and forgotten house, full of dim portraits and unpolished panelling, but it started to fall down in the nineteenth century. Today only a couple of gables and the watchtower survive, but the Ardernes' town house in Stockport survives in good shape – Underbank Hall; now a Bank.

Hyde Hall stands not far away (but in Lancashire), on a naturally defensive position overlooking the Tame. Today it is a relic island of farmland given over to 'Horseyculture' with lots of vainly weedkilled docks. The hall is fronted by its extensive farmyard, a fine big courtyard of farm buildings, mostly of brick, many of them dated. Over the farmyard archway is the delightful inscription MARY WOODIWIS 1839, but the place was of course built by the Hydes. The timber-framed, whitewashed hall is at the back of

the farmyard. Already described as 'rather tottery' in 1913, but then still full of nice furniture, it is even more tottery today. It was originally H-shaped but one cross-wing – the family wing at the high end – has gone. The porch is dated 1625 but most of it probably dates to the middle of the previous century, when so many Lancashire and Cheshire great houses were rebuilt. There were once two Hyde Halls; the other was in Hyde itself. The Hydes were a very numerous family, bearing the arms a chevron and three lozenges or on a field azure, and claiming kinship with the Earls of Clarendon. In a field beside our Hyde Hall there is a stranded wagon train. A long line of old railway wagons, wheel-less, weed-grown, and going nowhere. How symbolic can you get?

Denton Hall, sadly, has gone. It stood very close to the line of the M60, near Junction 24. It belonged to

Marple Hall Decline and Fall. This remarkable series of photographs was shot by Jack Wilkinson between 1940 and 1957. They record the sad and slow decline of Marple Hall – today no more than a grassed site.

the Holland family, and was built shortly before1500. Much of it disappeared as early as 1895, more in the 1930s. In 1979 the last bit, a remaining brick cross-wing, was taken down. It was nothing much to look at from outside, but the brick was just a casing added to a highly decorative timber-framed structure inside, with curly-tailed monsters carved on the braces of the tie-beams. The timber bits were rescued by Frank Smith and taken to Chonar Farm at Alderley Edge, where they were re-erected as a fancy barn for vintage cars. So something yet remains of Denton Hall, but in the wrong place.

Bredbury Hall is signposted off the M60 from the horrible Junction 25. It is not romantic, having been turned into a hotel and country club with a golf course attached. The hall is a plain white house with a Regency roof, enveloped by extensive building. Bredbury Hall does however have a beautifully romantic situation. The untamed river Goyt flows in front of the hotel block, an old oak tree clings to a big rock overhanging the water.

Goyt Hall is really pretty. A black-and-white house in a green setting – the perfect Cheshire recipe (yes, we are in Cheshire now). It is a fair walk from the M60, about a mile south from Bredbury Hall through increasingly verdant country, along the Goyt valley. Goyt Hall was built in about 1570 for Randle Davenport (initials RD on gable). It looks rather like the centre part of Wythenshawe Hall, as Wythenshawe must have looked before all its Georgian and Victorian extensions in fact. An H-shaped house, with a family wing at one end and a kitchen wing at the other. The middle part is not a medieval great hall but a more fashionable and comfortable two-storey range, with a great chamber upstairs. The right-hand cross-wing has been rebuilt in brick, but it matters surprisingly little because the basic shape of the house is not disturbed.

The loss of Marple Hall is perhaps the most bittersweet because the site is charged with great passions from the Civil War. The daughter of the Hall had the misfortune to fall in love with a Royalist. Her father, like many Cheshire gentry, was a Republican; a family servant took the hint and snicked the cavalier's saddle girths. He slid to his watery death while crossing the River Goyt. The spirit of his lover was said to haunt the Hall and banks of the River.

'And from the terrace of this ancient hall
The weird-like music trembles through the air
Sad and mournful yet divinely soft
As of a spirit in its last despair.'

A music perhaps heard no more - the Hall was finally demolished as unsafe in 1957. It had in fact been abandoned by its last owners, the Isherwood brothers, Christopher and Richard, from the 1940s onwards, and allowed to slide into ruin, assisted by vandalism. All that now remains is the lintel stone originally set up in 1658 at the time of England's Republican experiment 'and now looking uncannily like a gravestone'. On a visit to the empty site of the vanished Hall (from California) in the 1960s Christopher Isherwood is reported to have "felt no grimness or sadness" at seeing only grass where the house had stood "only wonderfully joyful". And yet one worrying footnote – a helmet and spurs, contemporary with the Civil War, were recovered here from the River Goyt in the nineteenth century... **PP**

A Fake Mill - Pear Mill is a landmark, whether you are sweeping round the southeast quadrant of the M60 or trundling across Stockport viaduct in a train. Seen against the Pennine foothills it is big and red, with yellow stripes, seven storeys high, multi-windowed, with a tall chimney, and bearing aloft on the top of its water tower an unmistakable dome in the shape of a glistening white pear.

Mills have not often been considered objects of beauty in the landscape. Rather perhaps symbols of unending toil, where people, called hands, were driven by the machinery and not vice versa. But now that the cotton mills of Manchester have stopped spinning cotton, and have been so drastically thinned out, we can begin to appreciate what a truly fine building Pear Mill is, splendid in its confidence and a perfect example of form following function.

It was designed by those kings of northern mill architecture, Stotts of Oldham, and built in 1907. Its vital statistics were the 137,312 mule spindles for medium to superfine cotton. It could have been twice the size. The west end is finished with a blank temporary wall, ready for expansion if required - but it never was.

Every mill had a name. The name had to be memorable, and it had to be short, so that it could be picked out in white brick in the chimney. Ace, Arrow, Beehive, Butts, Cairo, Don, Eclipse and so on. Sometimes the name lent itself to some modest theming. Here the pear motif can be seen not just on the tower top but at the corners of the chimney pedestal and on the corner turrets of the mill itself.

The heart of a mill was its engine house. Here was the huge steam engine, gleaming in its power and balletic in its motion. The engine at Pear Mill (made by George Saxon Ltd of Manchester) was one of the largest, rated at 4,500 horsepower. It turned a gigantic grooved flywheel at awesome speed, so perfectly balanced that its revolution was almost invisible, but creating a great wind. Endless ropes snaked up from the flywheel to drive the machines on each floor of the mill. The flywheel at Pear Mill was over four metres wide, with grooves for 73 ropes. A row of Lancashire boilers made the steam, and high in the air the smoke issuing from the chimney told the world that the mill was in business.

For a taste of mill engines in action leave the M60 at Junction 18 on the M62, eastbound to Junction 21 at Milnrow on a Sunday to visit Ellenroad Engine House. The bizarre situation there is that the engine house, boiler house and chimney are preserved in working order but the mill itself was demolished in 1985 (for the second time - the first mill burnt down in 1916). So coal is fed in, the boilers boil, the engines reciprocate and the flywheel spins and the 200ft chimney smokes - but all for nothing. **MH**

Above: Pear Mill. Pear Mill (built 1907) seen against the Pennine foothills. Seven storeys high, multi-windowed, with a tall chimney, and bearing aloft on the top of its water tower an unmistakable dome in the shape of a glistening white pear.

How did we get here? - To love or hate a modern or ancient building is understandable; to love or hate a motorway, which has no architect, no inhabitants and only a dubious paternity in Hitler's Autobahnen, may seem at first sight perverse.

The M60 is the only orbital motorway in Britain – London's 'Orbital' M25 is partly dual carriageway (Dartford Bridge and Tunnel) and hence does not qualify. Yet Manchester's Orbital differs radically from London's. The M25 was thrown up in one act of will in the eleven year period from 1986. Manchester's M60 was organic: it began with the construction of the Western Stretford-Eccles bypass in 1958 and it required over 40 years for the circle to be completed by the opening of the Middleton-Denton Eastern section.

Some will see in this long lapse of time the neglect that Westminster often shows for the needs of her provincial children. But the long lapse means that the M60 is a pocket history of motorway building in Britain. The M60 Motorway's several styles reflect changing perceptions of motorway philosophy –

be it crash barriers, sound baffles, landscaping or the concept of community severance ...

But the M60 Motorway is also a binding force, creating a new Greater Manchester. Locations are now inelegantly referred to as being inside or outside the M60 Motorway Box. This bonding of diverse places is also not without philosophical antecedents: in the 1880s and 1890s the planning and building of the Manchester Ship Canal (over which the M60 Motorway soars at Barton) was seen by many as a means for the integration of competing local interests (particularly those of the cities of Manchester and Salford) and for creating the idea of a Greater Manchester. The M60 Motorway may be seen in the same light: it has redefined the location of Manchester as being within the M60 area. La ville tentaculaire of the French Nineteenth century city poets has been given a framework of steel and concrete. The radiating city roads of La Ville Radieuse of Le Corbusier (1935) have arrived, not at their expected countryside, but at a circular man-made concrete limit.

The M60 Motorway is in fact only a new and vivid extension of those economic forces continuously at work in Manchester from as early as the 1850s, when pure manufacture of goods (principally, of course, cotton goods) gave way to warehousing and distribution. This change altered the very fabric of Manchester city centre, with giant warehouses constructed as renaissance palaces – the present Britannia Hotel, built as a warehouse by Watts, a Lord Mayor, is but one example. The M60 is the summation of this distribution process: a literal and visible hub with spokes, a physical manifestation of distribution theory, connecting Manchester with every part of Britain.

But where are our latter-day renaissance palaces ? Pre-fab aluminium and steel hulks in anonymous trailer parks. Manchester no longer builds in classical style. As one Manchester architect aptly phrased it: "She has long given up the attempt to force upon a commercial nineteenth century town, with a sunless and humid climate, the refinement and perfect beauty of the art of the Greeks in the golden age of Pericles" - unless of course we include the Trafford Centre...

The Naming of Parts

But it is curious that the M60 Motorway had no abiding identity until 1998. Before that it was the Eccles By-pass (M63) or sections of other motorways – the M62, which connected Liverpool to Hull, or the M63 to Stockport, or the M66 from Stockport to Denton. The final section from 12 o'clock to 3 o'clock, which completed the circle and allowed the new M60 name, was not built until 1998, when it cost another £8mn merely to replace all the signage with the new M60 brand. Over this long period another completely

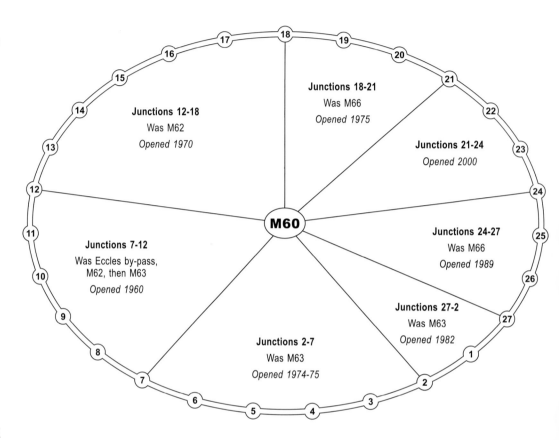

new eleven mile motorway from Eccles to Birch Services had been proposed (in 1993) and scrapped after public outcry (in 1995) – though not before 300 houses had been compulsorily purchased and then sold back. On the planners' books the M60 remains however still the *Manchester Outer Ring Road.*

Not only that: the M60 has another hidden name and function; it is part of the Trans European Road Network (TERN) E20 Euroroute, linking incongruously Shannon to St Petersburg, via ferries from Hull to Denmark, Sweden and Estonia. A strange dream to see Eccles, Swinton and Leningrad linked ...we really do not know what dreams the European motorway planners are dreaming for us in this, the new millennium. Perhaps best not to know.

Even if they dream, motorway planners do not permit themselves much romanticism in naming –

they merely number the junctions (there are 27 on the M60). Between the junctions are 'sections' – those on the M60 are comparatively foreshortened. The 'flawed section' between Junctions 12 and 13 of the M60 has the highest level of traffic on the whole of the phantom Euroroute E20; not surprisingly it is also an accident blackspot, renowned for its multiple shunts as motorists weave across the lanes. Average distance between junctions on the M60 is 1.3 miles (2.1km) – half that of the M25 at 3.7 miles (6.6km).

Greater Manchester's motorways, including the M60, saw some 5.8 billion vehicle kilometres in 2002 – about 6% of the UK total, and one of the highest for any area of its size. This translates into some 89,000 vehicles a day – or put another way: if you stood at the side of the M60, a vehicle would pass you every second of the day and night, all year round. There are many reasons for this density – not least that the North West also has the highest tonnage freighted by road in the UK, and many national distribution centres.

There are furthermore over a million vehicles registered in Greater Manchester – and 2.7 mn in the North West. If you are wondering if the standard of driving really has gone down, it is no reassurance to learn that one third of all those breathalysed by the police for alcohol are positive – nor that this figure has doubled over the past decade. Drug abuse is not yet tested, but must be of a similar magnitude.

Abiding Images

Some structures, such as administrative structures, are born impermanent: the Greater Manchester County, for example, around which much of the M60 now sweeps, had a brief life of only nine years from 1974 to 1983 – it has vanished, along with its coat of arms (the supporting lions had a book and a French horn at their shoulders – learning and music). It is hard to imagine the M60 being awarded a coat of arms for learning and music: but even a rose and three sheaves of wheat for Lancashire and Cheshire would be welcome. An identity.

What, then, might be the M60's abiding image? The image of Manchester was early delineated by the sad realism and poverty-sick matchstickmen of Lowry. Perhaps the M60 is characterised by what it has effaced – Fred Sowerbutt's Allotment and a complete reservoir at Audenshaw. Or by its unexplained absences: 'There are no services on the M60' – a chilling phrase, as though everyone is still hurrying home to a 1950s Mancunian teatime. Or perhaps the modern image is consumerism – the blue Roman folly of the Trafford Centre seen illuminated from the Motorway at night, approached past swathes of golf courses.

Or in the counter-culture, perhaps the image is the numerous and highly visible sewage lagoons and cemeteries of the Irwell and Mersey floodplains where all consumerism must itself be consumed. There are five major sewage works along the M60, Heathside at Junction 2, Castle Hill at Junction 25, while Eccles and Barton at Junction 11 are both beautifully visible from the Trafford Flyover on the Manchester Ship Canal, and can be detected on good days in Dumplington (a.k.a. The Trafford Centre). One omission: there are almost no car breakers' yards visible from the M60.

Right: Allotments at Brinnington overlooking the M60 motorway as it sweeps into the east side of Stockport near Junction 27. To the south of the motorway overlooking the town are blocks of flats built by the County Borough of Stockport and in the late 50's early 60's. The white building to the left is an office block on Wellington Rd South.

M60 & Greater Manchester: Key Facts

Population:	2.5mn
Roads:	5000 miles
Motorways:	85 miles
Cars:	6,00,00 trips per day
Buses:	700,00 trips per day
Trains:	70,000 local trips per day
Planes:	35,00 trips per day
Petrol:	1.2 tonnes per head
CO2:	32.0 mn tonnes per year
Waste:	4.4 tonnes per head per year

Adapted from Ravetz, City Region 2020

Perhaps in the end the image of the M60 is merely the new pattern the M60 has imposed on a transport network already ancient. Seen on the map, the M60 is a blue scalloped jelly mould, where the Motorway is forced to weave around the sinuous contours of the Irwell and Mersey floodplains. At Sale's weird Junction 7 the M60 uncannily cuts across all the motive possibilities known to man: a Roman trunk road (the A56 with its saxon 'Washway' and Stretford names), the Mersey River, the Bridgewater Canal, the Manchester to Altrincham railway line, now used by Metrolink trams and the Transpennine cycle track; it only narrowly misses a set of stepping stones in Sale Water Park. Even the power pylons march in sympathy alongside this junction.

This is the umbilical point of the M60 Motorway, where all the leylines and fengshui intersect – a place of raw and ancient energies. If Manchester is laid out like a Sleeping Goddess, as one mammary etymology of its name rather pointedly suggests, then this is her geomantic navel. And her troubled head rests in the Garden at Prestwich County Asylum, next to Junction 17. Other vital organs may be detected below.

Motorway Policy in the North

It comes as a shock to discover that before 1937 there was no national roads plan in a small country the size of Britain. Indeed the Royal Commission on transport of 1928 had cast doubt on even the need for inter-city road improvements. In 1936 the Institution of Highway Engineers produced its own plan for some 2,800 miles of motorway. Lobbying followed in 1937 as a high-level junket of 225 MPs and local officials to Hitler's Germany as part of a 'German Roads Delegation' cannily funded by the British Road Federation. The Ministry of Transport did not concur with the views of the participants, and an MoT official wrote somewhat tartly:

'Among the personal attributes of the rulers of Germany... is a mania for speed, which has found its expression in motor roads. There seems no reason why this country [Britain], with its different traditions, should blindly copy at the behest of a delegation led by the Chairman of the Cement Manufacturer's Association.'

In any event, the Second World War, and the irritating personal manias of the rulers of Germany naturally stopped any British motorway plans. After the war a plan was finally drafted by the Ministry, but this languished until 1960 when the MoT at last produced its official 'Master Plan' incorporating 1000 miles of new motorways. Lancashire was quicker off the mark than the rest of the country, and pushed for an experimental 62 mile (99 km.) stretch of motorway which eventually became the M6.

In 1961 Manchester obtained a local Act of Parliament to acquire land and property to build new roads - the 'City Centre', 'Inner', 'Intermediate' and 'Outer' Ring Roads. Manchester Centre still bears the scars of these proposals, with some buildings set back from the existing road line for the eventual (non)-arrival of a three lane highway. Indeed Watts Warehouse (now the Britannia Hotel) and built by Lord Mayor Watts of Abney Hall, was to have been demolished.

There was to a roundabout the size of four football pitches in the City Centre, at the junction of Princess and Portland Street. Pedestrians were to be shipped up to a first floor deck level - which still exists around parts of the University Precinct on Oxford Road. These proposals fortunately languished in the planners' inbox.

1968 : The Manchester Rapid Transit Study (MRTS)
There was a sense by 1968, at the time of the Manchester Rapid Transit Study that bus services to and in the city centre were deteriorating. Road congestion, it was estimated, would not allow more than 25-30% of people to get to work by car. If this problem of public transport were not solved, the Study stated, then 'the future prosperity of Central Manchester as a regional centre of employment will decline.'

That report looked at an overhead monorail for Manchester (for example the driverless Westinghouse 'Skybus') and rejected it on the grounds of noise and visual intrusion, in favour of a Duorail – the modern Metrolink, because of its more favourable cost, reliability and compatibility with the existing suburban rail network. However, the Second Millennium has now come and gone and the Trafford Centre and Manchester Airport are still not connected by anything, even a Skybus.

There is also one glaring omission from the terms of reference of MRTS – there is no coverage of the Motorway system, no concept that through traffic might be diverted from crossing the city, and no proposal to link other transport systems to the Motorway. The MRTS remit extends only to 7_ miles out of Manchester. There is also no discussion of out-of-town shopping (Cheadle Royal and the Trafford Centre) nor indeed of the potential growth of mass tourism abroad through Manchester Airport. The whole focus is on maintaining the vitality of the city centre, in the face of declining industry and the migration of private housing to Cheshire and North Manchester.

One North-South difference was very notable: large Northern cities continued to pursue large urban motorway plans after their benefits had been questioned elsewhere. There was lower car ownership in these cities than in the South, and fewer people understood that a programme of road building did not alleviate congestion. Opposition in the South had been led by an articulate urban middle class; the dominant class in Northern inner cities was often the working class, renting council property. Local councils therefore had little trouble driving through roads, with compulsory demolitions. Consequently, northern cities with lower car ownership tended, perversely, to get the highest mileage of new urban roads.

Where does the M60 signage go from here?
From July 2000 we have been in that strange country, the Government's 10 Year Transport Plan. Its target was to reduce inter-urban congestion by 5%, but this was abandoned in 2002 – traffic is now expected to rise by 15% by 2010, lorries to increase in number, and to get bigger and heavier, and private motor car use to increase. Most sensible projections conclude that the M60 has at most bought us three years or so before congestion again eats into the benefits. Hence the plethora of secondary initiatives and widening schemes.

For example, the M60 is fortunate, now that it exists, to have the spotlight of a Highways Agency Route Management Strategy (RMS) focused on its shiny tarmac. The RMS began in October 2003, and was completed by Autumn 2004. The RMS terms of reference include 'delivery of a ten year vision for the road and of the improvements the HA would like to make'. This will be interesting to watch. Two or more governments will have vanished in that time frame.

'The air is full of noises

....that give delight but hurt not.' Hardly. Motorways are renowned for their generation of noise and the M60 is no exception. A level of 57 decibels is defined as the onset of community annoyance. If you stand next to any exposed section of the M60, even if it is in a cutting, you can expect to absorb around 80 decibels – and even at a distance of 350 feet (113 meters) this will only fall to 70 decibels – above the annoyance level. It requires a 10 foot (3 meter) high barrier to make a real impact – the sound still only falls away to around 60 decibels. There are other criteria – commercial vehicles are noisier than cars; engine and exhaust noises are greater than tyre noise on inclines. Noise seems greater at night.

There is, strangely enough, also a concept of 'tranquil areas' with its own definition: anyone within 3 km of a motorway, or 1km of a road which is difficult to cross, is unlikely to live in a 'tranquil area' or to be able to avoid traffic noise. In effect, most of Manchester within the M60 Motorway box, and for some way around its perimeter, lacks tranquility.

Wider still, and wider: I tolled you so.

Now that the Trafford Centre is open (1998) and also Manchester Airport Runway 2 (2000), the M60 shows no sign of being able to cope with all the traffic it has generated, so an obvious solution is widening to allow it to generate yet more. Indeed a pathetic aside for the Department of Transport on widening as late as 1993 stated – 'Eventually traffic growth will slow down and cease.' Presumably shortly after the good intention road to hell is tarmaced over. The M60 now has the second highest flow of vehicles at peak in the UK, after the M25, at 174,000 an hour. There have been two major M60 improvement schemes – widening between Junctions 5 and 8 on both sides – at £100mn+ and running to Spring 2006; and a proposal to widen between Junctions 15 to 13 anti-clockwise.

There is also the JETTS proposal (pencilled in for 2008 to 2011; cost £479mn) to deal with the problems of Junctions 12 to 18 – Eccles to Whitefield. Consultants initially recommended separation of long distance M62 traffic from local M60 traffic by redesigning the M60 to provide segregated lanes, but this seems unlikely. Instead 'Active Traffic Management' will be instituted. New slip roads will be constructed to bypass Junction 12, with some localised widening, and variable speed limits enforced by cameras. But the long-term solution is seen as the introduction of road user charging within Greater Manchester after 2011. The JETTS report pulls no punches: "A flat rate toll is a sensible 'stick' to encourage greater use of public transport, by targeting those most likely to be able to switch mode."

Envoi and Convoy

Enough. We know the outcome. More FWDs, bullbar to bullbar. More LGVs and HGVs with left-hand drivers. The M60 Motorway is its own sufficient paradox: a way to avoid, not enter, the City of Manchester. It converts radial into orbital movement. It does not go from A to B – it goes in a disturbing circle of A to A, clockwise or counter-clockwise. It is a daily and nightly transient mass of Mancunian humanity, on an abiding physical structure. You can never drive onto the same M60 Motorway twice. Its destinations are the letters tattooed onto the whitening knuckles of Everymotorist as they grip their steering wheel: love, and hate. **PP**

M60 Motorway Junctions 27 to 2 *(Formerly M63 Stockport East-West By-pass)* -

Work started on the first of two contracts in June 1979, followed by the second, in February 1980. The By-pass was completed and opened to traffic in July 1982.

Next Page: Stockport Railway Viaduct over the River Mersey in the 1840s, looking Northeast. Mills and trains powered by steam and coal dominate this scene, but an older source of power can be seen in the windmill on Lancashire Hill at top left. The line of the houses through the viaduct show how the railways began the process of severance which the M60, running through its northern arches, will perpetuate.

By September 1974, the completion of Sale Eastern and Northenden By-pass, together with Sharston By-pass, had extended the M63 as far as Cheadle Heath. The need for its continuation, therefore, by the early construction of the of the 2 mile long Stockport East-West By-pass, became increasingly important, not only as part of the Manchester Outer Ring Road but also as a means of relieving the A560, within the town.

L G Mouchel and Partners, Consulting Engineers, were appointed by the Department of Transport to undertake its design and subsequent supervision of construction. From Cheadle Road, the proposed By-pass was to pass under the slip road connecting it to the A560, and continue alongside a sewage disposal works, before passing under a railway line and over the River Mersey. It then ran close to the Glazebrook-Godley Railway Line, and through disused sidings to a two-level interchange at Travis Brow, with connections to the A6. Continuing under both the arches of the viaduct which carried the main Manchester-Crewe Railway, and the A6, it was to pass through the site of a former railway station before crossing the River Tame. The By-pass was to terminate at a two-level interchange at the junction of Tiviot Way, the A560, and Brinnington Road, Portwood.

A total of 13 bridges and 3 pedestrian subways was required. The bridge carrying the Cheadle Exchange Railway Line over the By-pass was to be a four-span reinforced concrete structure designed, and the construction supervised, by British Rail. The River Mersey Bridge was designed with three-spans, of 50 feet, 100 feet and 50 feet, and a continuous post-

tensioned pre-stressed concrete superstructure, at a 45° skew. The route of the By-pass occupied part of the bed of the River Mersey, which it was necessary to divert between retaining walls. On the north side, the wall was to be 200 feet long and 40 feet high and on the south side, 500 feet long and 25 feet high. The scheme for the dual three-lane carriageway By-pass was the subject of a Public Inquiry in 1977. A favourable decision enabled work to start on the first of two contracts, in June 1979 followed by the second, in February 1980.

Large areas of land required for the By-pass had been cleared by Stockport Borough Council under slum-clearance provisions. The works involved the demolition of over 100 houses and shops, 18 industrial premises, five public houses, a petrol station and three car showrooms. The construction of the By-pass through the urban area entailed a number of unusual features.

Some 35,000 cubic yards of sewage sludge from the works at Cheadle Heath, had to be removed to a site at Altrincham. St. Mary's Church and School, are immediately north and about 80 feet above the level of the By-pass, which is in a deep cutting at that point. The lower 50 feet is in sandstone rock and the soft ground above it is retained by a contiguous piled brick-faced wall held by ground anchors. East of Lancashire Hill and in order to minimise the land-take, the By-pass is contained within reinforced-earth retaining walls, with pre-cast concrete facings.

The Main Line Railway Viaduct is a dominant feature within the centre of the town. Designed by George Watson Buck, it was completed in 1840 and is reputed to be the largest brick-built viaduct in the Country. As the By-pass was designed to pass through two of the spans, in shallow cutting, it was necessary to underpin the foundations of one of the piers in order to ensure adequate support.

Major service diversions were required. Much of this work had a great influence on the construction sequence. A6 is a main traffic artery and its importance was recognised by a requirement in the relevant Contract, that it must be kept open at all times. It was necessary for the existing Wellington Road Bridge carrying the A6 to be replaced and a temporary bridge was constructed, which was also used for diverted services.

The carriageway construction in the western of the two Contracts is a continuous reinforced concrete pavement, except over the River Mersey Bridge. Elsewhere, the carriageways are of conventional flexible construction with a wearing course of hot rolled asphalt.

The By-pass was completed and opened to traffic in July 1982.

M60 Motorway Junctions 2 to 7 *(Formerly: M63 Sale Eastern and Northenden By-pass, and Sharston By-pass)* - Work began on this section in May 1971 and this was followed by the main contract in February 1972. The Sale Eastern and Northenden By-pass was opened to traffic in September 1974. The M63 section of Sharston By-pass, together with the Kingsway Interchange, was however completed in January 1974 and the remainder in May 1975.

Work began on this section in May 1971 and this was followed by the main contract in February 1972. The Sale Eastern and Northenden By-pass was opened to traffic in September 1974. The M63 section of Sharston By-pass, together with the Kingsway Interchange, was however completed in January 1974 and the remainder in May 1975.

The construction of the section of the M62 Lancashire-Yorkshire Motorway between Worsley and Whitefield had formed, in effect, part of the proposed Manchester Outer Ring Road, as a north easterly extension of the Stretford Eccles By-pass.

Progress around the southern and eastern parts of the periphery of the conurbation was, however, much slower, with programming largely influenced by financial restraints. The principle of constructing a series of local By-passes to form elements of the Ring Road was, therefore, adopted. Sale Eastern and Northenden By-pass, together with Sharston By-pass were such schemes.

Prior to 1967, the design of the Sale Eastern and Northenden By-pass was the responsibility of the three highway authorities through whose areas the road would pass, namely the Manchester City

Council, which employed G Maunsell and Partners as Consulting Engineers, and the Lancashire and Cheshire County Councils. When the Ring Road became a Trunk Road, responsibility was transferred to the North Western Road Construction Unit of the Department of the Environment, with the design of the 4 miles of the route from Stretford to north of the Glazebrook-Godley railway line in Gatley shared by the Lancashire and Cheshire Sub Units of the North Western Road Construction Unit and by G Maunsell & Partners.

The obvious route for the By-pass was through the mainly undeveloped corridor of the River Mersey Valley. Several possible alternatives were investigated before the decision was taken to adopt an alignment along the southern edge of the Valley, skirting the residential development. This route was found to be the most economic and one which kept, to the minimum, disturbance to property, and the recreational areas in the Valley, consistent with the need for a standard of design appropriate to a motorway.

From the end of the Stretford-Eccles By-pass, the motorway would cross over Chester Road (A56), the River Mersey, the Bridgewater Canal and the Manchester-Altrincham electrified railway line. Continuing in a south eastwards direction, it would be generally on embankment through to the crossing of Princess Parkway a major radial route, formerly built to near urban motorway standards, and serving the City of Manchester.

The main engineering problem in deciding to build a motorway through the Mersey Valley - partly across the actual flood plain of the river - was the need to keep above the flood level of the river. In order to achieve this, the motorway had to be built mainly on high embankment with only short lengths in cutting.

The flood plain itself is made up of post-glacial materials such as normally consolidated alluvium and terrace gravels. Below the recent deposits, the 'solid' rocks of the Triassic system were found at depths of from less than 20 feet to more than 60 feet. The measures necessary to deal with these recent deposits were important features of the project: on the one hand how to use them as a source of fill and, on the other, how to construct an embankment up to 40 feet high without causing failure either to the embankment or to the very weak alluvium below.

In addition there was the problem of finding some 2 million cubic yards of material which would need to be imported. If it had been brought in from sources outside the site, the result would have been large numbers of heavy lorries transporting material along already congested local roads.

It was proposed, therefore, that material for the embankments should be excavated from an area between the motorway and the River Mersey known as the Sale Ees, and the use of this material resulted in substantial savings in cost. The excavation was to be permanently filled with water from the river, with the intention that the Greater Manchester Council and Trafford Borough Council would develop it for recreational purposes. It also would provide the Mersey and Weaver River Unit with increased flood storage capacity.

On Sale Ees, large scale laboratory tests showed that a skeletal system of vertical sand drains would accelerate settlement of the motorway embankment and reduce both the amount of temporary overfilling and the period for which it would be required. An advance contract was carried out to provide this 'skeleton' and install the system of piezometers necessary to measure the pressure of the groundwater in the soil beneath the embankment, and to control the rate of its construction so that there was no risk of a slip occurring in the soil beneath.

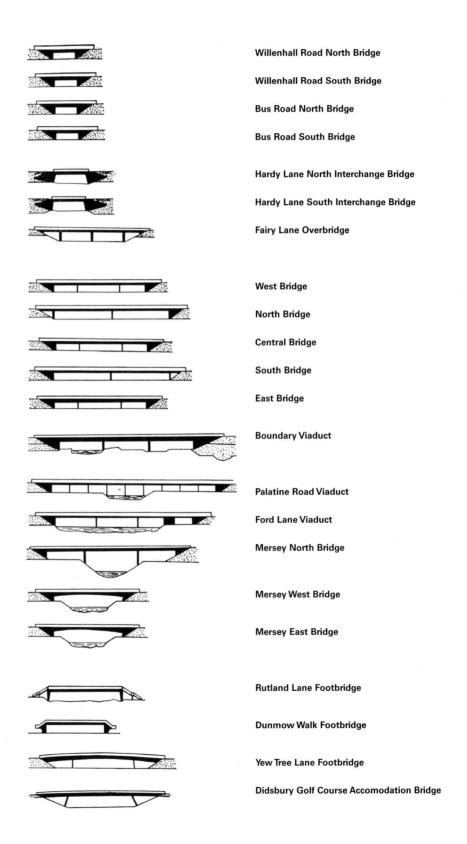

Willenhall Road North Bridge

Willenhall Road South Bridge

Bus Road North Bridge

Bus Road South Bridge

Hardy Lane North Interchange Bridge

Hardy Lane South Interchange Bridge

Fairy Lane Overbridge

West Bridge

North Bridge

Central Bridge

South Bridge

East Bridge

Boundary Viaduct

Palatine Road Viaduct

Ford Lane Viaduct

Mersey North Bridge

Mersey West Bridge

Mersey East Bridge

Rutland Lane Footbridge

Dunmow Walk Footbridge

Yew Tree Lane Footbridge

Didsbury Golf Course Accomodation Bridge

Right: Bridges of the Sale
Eastern and Northenden
By-Pass M63, 1972-74
Now M60 Motorway
Junctions 5 To 7)

Another technical problem inherent in planning a motorway through the Valley was the need for repeated crossings of the River. The route chosen on the south side involved fewer points of crossing then any alternative but, even so, it crossed the course of the River five times. However, by diverting a loop of the River near Didsbury Golf Course, clear of the motorway, the need for two of these crossings was removed with a considerable saving in cost. This diversion was carried out in advance of the motorway construction by the Mersey and Weaver River Authority. Three interchanges were required, at Chester Road (A56) in Stretford, at the Hardy Lane Extension in Sale, and at Princess Parkway (A5103). The By-pass required the construction of 35 bridges, various culverts and retaining walls and a piled raft.

The principal bridges forming the Princess Parkway Interchange were of either single or double spine box post-tensioned structures. The requirement that there should be no bridge piers in the central reserve of Princess Parkway, resulted in the main spans of the crossing being of the order of 115 feet.

The Palatine Road viaduct has eight and nine spans carrying the west and east bound carriageways of the motorway over Palatine Road and the River Mersey.

The first major contract, undertaken in advance, included the construction of two slip roads and a fly-over bridge in the Chester Road Interchange, and bridges over the Mersey Overflow Channel. Work began in May 1971 and this was followed by the main Contract in February 1972.

Meanwhile advance works for the construction of Sharston By-pass had also begun. This scheme, designed by Howard Humphreys & Sons, Consulting Engineers, was primarily designed to relieve Sharston by removing traffic from several major traffic routes passing through the area. It was, however, an important element in the further development of the M63.

The first of the two main contracts began in January 1972. The most significant feature was the construction of the major Kingsway Interchange which provides a junction between M63, M56 and the A34 (Kingsway) a main radial route between central Manchester and the South.

To the west of the Interchange a half-mile section of motorway completed the Sale Eastern and Northenden By-pass and, to the east, the M63 was extended for a length of over a mile to a junction with the A560.

The major part of Sharston By-pass, however, connecting with the Bowdon-Wythenshaw Section of the M56, formed the eastern end of that motorway. The western half of this two mile length of the By-pass was constructed under a further contract extending from a two-level interchange at the junction with Sharston Road. Works in this contract began some 12 months later to enable the re-siting of various business premises, mostly shops.

Extensive bridge engineering was involved, much of it concentrated at the Kingsway Interchange. The majority of the 27 bridges required, had to be designed as 'one-off' structures because of the restricted nature of the site, with little scope for standardisation.

A major bridge was needed to carry the dual-carriageway Kingsway, widened by slip roads, over the M63 and slip roads. It had to be constructed on the line of Kingsway with as little disruption as possible to the heavy commuter traffic. This was achieved by designing and constructing the four-span bridge in separate 75 feet and 40 feet widths. The decks are continuous in-situ reinforced concrete slabs, carried on pre-cast reinforced concrete columns which were, in turn, placed in 5 feet

Above: Railway to Manchester Airport Railway bridge carrying the line from Manchester to Styal and Manchester Airport across Junctions 3 and 4 of the M60 (formerly M63), and Junction 1 of the M56 Motorways.

diameter cased holes on top of piles. The abutments are formed by concrete faced contiguous reinforced concrete bored piles. This method of construction obviated the need to complete the full depths of general excavation before completion of the structure, with consequent considerable temporary support works.

A ten-span viaduct was designed to carry the south-east slip road over the motorway, the west-south and west-north slip roads, and Kingsway. It is a continuous trapezoidal spine box girder composite with an RC deck slab which cantilevers each side of the box. The bridge is on a horizontal curve of a radius of 500 feet, and the deck is supported on single rectangular reinforced concrete cantilever columns with flared heads, enlarged below ground and supported on spread footings. The end supports are three-leg reinforced concrete skeletal abutments with cantilevered reinforced concrete return wing walls.

The bridge carrying the M56 over the Cheadle link railway line, and the M63 over the Glazebrook-Godley railway line and the eastbound carriageway of the M56, both have a skew of 61°. The decks are of reinforced concrete, composite with steel Universal

Beams spanning square between the abutments and pier in the centre, and steel box girders in the triangular edge areas.

The bridge carrying the Styal railway line over the motorway, was designed by British Rail and constructed under their supervision. This is a three-span continuous pre-stressed concrete through girder bridge with 8 foot deep edge beams. The complete deck was built alongside the track and launched sideways into position in a single track possession, the excavation under the bridge taking place subsequently.

The Merrison Committee's interim report on box girder bridges was published after the bridge designs had been completed and the contract was about to go out to tender. This required a complete reappraisal of the steel box girder bridges resulting in some design modifications which were completed by the contract starting date. The high motorway embankments adjacent to the bridge carrying the M63 over the Glazebrook-Godley railway line are situated in the flood plain, where a layer of alluvium was found in the initial soil survey at depths varying from 5 to 15 feet. Preliminary studies indicated that the placing of embankments over 20 feet in height would require extra care. Piezometers to control the rate of construction were installed under the embankments and provision was made for varying rates of placement fill. The fill material used in the embankment up to flood level about 10 feet in height was free draining and, above that, pulverised fuel ash (PFA) was used as a lightweight filling. Approximately 750,000 cubic yards of material was excavated and placed in embankments and some 550,000 cubic yards of material was imported as filling to embankments.

The Sale Eastern and Northenden By-pass was opened to traffic in September 1974. The M63 section of Sharston By-pass, together with the Kingsway

Interchange, was however completed in January 1974 and the remainder, in May 1975.

2003 Widening Scheme.
In March 2003 the AMEC-Alfred McAlpine joint venture was awarded a £102 million design and build contract to improve the section of the M60 between Junction 5 at Northern Moor and Junction 8 at Stretford. The joint venture will finalise design details before starting work in July 2003 with completion due by February 2006. The 7.4 kilometre section of motorway - which is currently part two lane and part three lane - will be widened by one lane in each direction with the addition of a parallel link road between Junction 6 and 8, to reduce congestion on both the motorway and local road network.

In addition to widening the motorway, the existing parallel link road between Junctions 7 and 8 will be extended to Junction 6 to improve safety and traffic flow for vehicles along this section. The four existing junctions will also all be improved.

M60 Motorway Junctions 7 to 13 *(Formerly: M63 Stretford Eccles By-pass and Carrington Spur)* - The construction of the 5 mile By-pass, which included a total of 22 bridges, started in April 1957 when work began on the first of several contracts. When the By-pass, at that time numbered M62, was opened in October 1960 it represented another 'first' for Lancashire - the first 'county motorway' in Britain in that the County Council was the Highway Authority, not the Minister of Transport.

The Spur was opened to traffic as the A6144 (M) in October 1987, 10 months ahead of schedule. As a single carriageway non-trunk motorway, with two-way traffic, it too was, to some extent, unique.

Although the completion of the M6 was a priority, the Lancashire County Council had given early attention to the needs of the other parts of the County where there were serious traffic problems. The 1949 Road Plan had identified the western sector of a proposed Manchester Outer Ring Road as one of the Express Routes to be constructed as a motorway, to bypass Stretford and Eccles and to serve the large Trafford Park industrial area.

It would also relieve the Barton swing-bridge which carried the busy A575 across the Manchester Ship Canal and where serious traffic delays occurred when the bridge was closed to allow shipping movements. Therefore, the main feature was to be a high-level bridge carrying the motorway over the Canal. As the A575 was a Class 1 road the By-pass was eligible for a 75 per cent Government grant and, in 1953, it was included in the programme of grant-aided schemes.

In the same year a nearby steelworks was having difficulty in finding a disposal site for its slag and the County Council, therefore, made arrangements for this to be tipped and compacted on the site of the south approach embankment of the proposed bridge. A Public Inquiry into the proposal had been held, but the work was actually carried out in advance of the Minister's decision. In that a favourable decision might not have been forthcoming, the County Council undoubtedly took a risk in proceeding with this work at such an early stage. It would, however, have been economic to re-excavate the embankment and move the material to another site, instead of paying the cost of importing fresh material from other sources and the, not unreasonable County Council's view, was that the Minister was certain to give his assent. By using some 400,000 tons of 'free' material nearly £100,000 was eventually saved. This embankment, which was completed at insignificant cost, was the first physical step in the construction of a motorway anywhere in Britain - even in advance of Preston By-pass.

With four intermediate interchanges, giving an average spacing of only 1_ miles, this was probably the first urban motorway in the Country. Standards for such roads had not yet been determined but, as some sections of the route passed through residential areas, the need to reduce land acquisition to a minimum was recognised in the designs which were adopted.

The County Council's traffic forecasts indicated that dual three-lane carriageways were needed, but the Ministry would only countenance the issue of grant for a dual two-lane scheme. The County Council,

therefore, had no alternative but to proceed accordingly. The construction of the 5 mile By-pass, which included a total of 22 bridges, started in April 1957 when work began on the first of several contracts.

Although shorter than Thelwall Viaduct, the 2425 feet long 18 span High Level Bridge was similar in many respects. With a maximum gradient on the approaches of 1 in 25 and rising to a height of some 100 ft above the level of the Canal, the piers varied in height from 30 to 80 feet above ground level. The superstructure consisted of eight steel plate girders of riveted construction carrying a reinforced concrete deck. The major part of the splicing of the girders was carried out prior to lifting into position.

The length of the main span crossing the Canal was 310 feet comprising two cantilevers each of 77 feet 6 inches carrying a simply supported 155 feet long centre suspended span. The anchor arm spans were 175 feet long. On the South side of the Canal, sections of the anchor arm and cantilever girders were lifted individually and supported on temporary trestles. Regrettably, the trestles formed of tubular steel scaffolding collapsed under the load and several lives were lost. Military trestling was used in subsequent operations.

A different method was employed on the North side in that each anchor arm and cantilever girder was spliced on the ground and lifted into position on the main pier. The steelwork sub-Contractor had been experiencing serious difficulties due to the demands of a militant group of his steel erectors, to the extent that he was forced into liquidation. Four of the girders had been erected and jacks were in position to enable fine adjustments to be made in line and level, in order that bracings could be fitted. The main Contractor appointed a replacement sub-Contractor but, unfortunately, the arrangements for the 'hand-over' proved to have been unsatisfactory.

A jacking operation was undertaken which caused the girders to fall over and several fatalities occurred. The Inquest which followed not only examined the cause of death but also considered the responsibilities of the various parties involved in the Contract. In that respect, it was a 'test case' and led to some of the early Health and Safety legislation affecting the construction industry. Neither the County Council as the Employer, not the County Surveyor as the Engineer under the Contract, were held to be in anyway responsible for the accidents. Whereas in the case of the Thelwall Viaduct, the suspended span girders were lifted into position using a crane on the tip of the cantilevers, at Barton, a Bailey bridge launching nose was used. The accidents caused a delay in the completion of the By-pass.

In one respect the delay was fortuitous. Steelworks slag from a different source to that used on the south approach to the Bridge had been utilised in the construction of embankments in the Northern part of the By-pass. Prior to the final surfacing being carried out, it was found that the carriageway formation had 'heaved' and investigations showed that this was due to the ingress of water causing the particular slag to swell. During the period of delay, the effect dissipated and a stable formation was achieved before the surfacing was completed. Mining subsidence of up to twelve feet was expected and provision was therefore made for the decks of the bridges carrying the motorway over the Bridgewater Canal to be capable of being jacked-up to maintain the required headroom.

At the Public Inquiry objections had been made to the northern terminal roundabout at Worsley, because of the perceived detrimental effect on the surroundings. On completion of the work, however, the County Council received a Civic Trust award for the design and landscape treatment. When the By-pass, at that time numbered M62, was opened in October 1960 it represented another 'first' for Lancashire - the first 'county motorway' in Britain in that the County Council was the Highway Authority, not the Minister of Transport.

In the 1970s, the Ring Road south of the Eccles Interchange was re-designated M63, with this interchange numbered as Junction 1.

The Carrington Industrial Complex lies to the west of the motorway, and on the south side of the Ship Canal. For many years, serious concern had been expressed at the movement of heavy goods vehicles, some carrying hazardous substances, on residential roads in Ashton-on-Mersey, Flixton, Davyhulme and West Sale. It was, however, February 1986 before work began on a contract for the construction of a 1 mile length of motorway, known as the Carrington Spur.

In order to provide a connection to the M63, it was necessary to construct an interchange, including Hallam Farm Bridge crossing over the heavily trafficked live motorway. The 100 feet long single span pre-cast pre-stressed concrete beam and slab bridge was to be supported on a reinforced concrete substructure on piled foundations. Designated as the new Junction 6 of the M63, the works also included a link road running parallel to it on each side. The provision of additional lanes north of this junction was the first Stage in the upgrading to dual three-lane carriageway standard. Ground conditions along the line of the Spur were poor and nearly 50,000 cubic yards of peat was removed and replaced with selected fill. Elsewhere vertical drains were installed under a 2 feet thick drainage blanket to accelerate consolidation of the alluvium flood plain.

Special measures were taken to protect and monitor the movement of a high pressure processed fuel pipeline which crossed the site at five locations. This collects refined petroleum products from refineries at Milford Haven and Fawley for distribution throughout the Midlands and the Manchester area.

A two-span continuous composite steel and concrete bridge crossing the River Mersey, a footbridge and an underpass, together with steel sign gantries, were also required. The design and supervision of the works was undertaken by the Manchester, Salford and Wigan Major Highways Consortium on behalf of Trafford Metropolitan Borough Council and the Department of Transport. The Spur was opened to traffic as the A6144 (M) in October 1987, 10 months ahead of schedule. As a single carriageway non-trunk motorway, with two-way traffic, it was, to some extent, unique. It was, however, intended that, in due course, it would be extended to the south and west and upgraded to meet the requirements of future development.

The second Stage in the upgrading of the M63 involved the widening and improvement of the section between Junctions 1 and 3. This included the Barton High Level Bridge which, by the early 80's was carrying traffic flows of 75,000 vehicles per day, some 50% in excess of the road's design capacity. Hold-ups at peak times were common due, in part, to the restraint imposed on heavy vehicles by the relatively steep approaches.

In 1967 the Ring Road had been designated a 'Trunk Road' and the Department of Transport appointed Mott Hay and Anderson, Consulting Engineers, to undertake the design and the supervision of the widening of the Bridge.

In order to provide dual three-lane carriageways and hard shoulders, an additional welded steel plate girder was to be erected on each side of the existing deck. These were to be supported on new rectangular hollow reinforced concrete piers carried on large diameter bored piles. The original 9 inch thick reinforced concrete deck was to be totally replaced and to be continuous across the full width of the bridge. Additional cross bracing was to be installed between the existing central girders to provide continuity.

The design and supervision of work on the other bridges in the interchange at Peel Green (Junction 2) was undertaken by Ward Ashcroft and Partners. This firm of Consulting Engineers was also responsible for the road works. The reconstruction of Barton Old Hall Railway Bridge carrying the Manchester to Liverpool main line over the M63, was also necessary and this was carried out by British Rail Engineering.

The High Level Bridge is a major crossing of the Ship Canal and there are few suitable alternative routes available. The Contract, which was awarded in March 1986, included a series of detailed traffic management schemes. These were aimed at maximising the use of the motorway during the construction, whilst at the same time allowing the Contractor the necessary possession and lane closures to carry out the very complex and difficult work. The Contract was completed in December 1988 and together with the other stages of the widening, and the construction of further By-passes referred to elsewhere, the M63 then had a dual three-lane carriageway standard as far as Portwood, beyond Stockport.

M60 Motorway Junctions 12 to 18 *(Formerly: M60 Eccles to Middleton Link, formerly part of M62)* - During the 1930's the need for a fast road route across the Pennines had been the subject of much discussion between the highway authorities in Lancashire and Yorkshire.

It was eventually agreed that it would be an extension of the East Lancashire Road, but little positive action was taken before the War, except for the reservation of land for the future construction of an all-purpose road, then known as the Yorkshire Branch Road.

Although the route was included in the 1949 Road Plan for Lancashire, it was not until 1961 that the Ministry of Transport invited the County Councils of Lancashire and the West Riding to survey and recommend a route for the motorway. Reconnaissance on foot was followed by an aerial survey of the whole area and extensive traffic surveys were carried out on both sides of the Pennines. Meteorological data was also examined to identify the alignment which would be least affected by fog, snow and high winds. The M60 section of the Lancashire Yorkshire Motorway presented the design engineers with the task of finding a route through urban areas in the west and north of the Manchester conurbation with its residential property and old industrial workings, and a network of roads, railways, canals and rivers to be crossed.

A study of existing records showed that the geology of the section from Eccles to Milnrow lies on the fringe of the Lancashire plain. Almost the whole of this area is covered by a blanket of glacial deposits and several peat mosses. West of the River Irwell (junction 16), coal measures had been extensively worked and further subsidence seemed unlikely, but to the east of the river the coalfield was still being exploited. Significant subsidence could therefore be expected, both during construction of the motorway and after it was opened to traffic.

Traffic forecasts indicated that dual three-lane carriageways would be necessary. The widths of the strips of land which had been reserved since the 1930's in urban areas such as Prestwich were, therefore, quite inadequate and unfortunately more than one hundred houses had to be demolished and the residents re-housed.

Prior to the formation of the Road Construction Unit, all the contracts for the construction of the motorway were awarded by the County Council. These included several advance works contracts, the first of which began in March 1966. The principal aim was the building of bridges at key locations in order to provide access for construction traffic along the line of motorway, thereby avoiding the use of existing roads, particularly in the urban areas.

The East Lancashire Road A580 was lowered up to a maximum depth of 50 feet and involved the driving of a 54 inch diameter segmented tunnel outfall 310 yards in length to provide drainage. This work was necessary in order to allow for the construction of Wardley Hall Bridge carrying the motorway over the A580 at the optimum vertical profile. A major structure of eight 120 feet long spans, it was designed to cope with the possibility of future settlement arising from the existence of old mine workings in close proximity to the site.

The bridge over the River Irwell has a single skew span of 200 feet. Ground conditions revealed the existence of an active geological fault - The Pendleton Fault - and underlying shallow coal measures. Although it was founded on rock and it was not anticipated that there would be any major problems, old tunnels were encountered.

These had been dug by Brindley to dewater early collieries which had functioned at the turn of the 18th century. Steel box girders supporting a reinforced concrete slab provided a stiff lightweight deck capable of speedy and safe erection and be able to withstand the predicted ground movements.

In May 1968 work began on a series of main contracts. They were all awarded by the Road Construction Unit, with the exception of that for the section between Worsley Court House and the A580. As a 1 mile extension of the Stretford-Eccles By-pass, the scheme was undertaken by the County Council and financed with a 100% grant from the Ministry as a potential trunk road motorway.

Two bridges, designed by British Rail, carried railways over the motorway the largest being at Besses o' the' Barn. This bridge forms the upper level of a three-level crossing comprising a railway, an all-purpose road and the motorway. The Manchester-Bury two-track railway line is carried at a considerable skew on a three-span pre-stressed concrete structure and is articulated to cater for anticipated severe subsidence due to coal mining.

The Trunk Roads Act of 1936 had transferred to the Minister the responsibility for the major national routes. With a few exceptions, none of the roads within the County Boroughs was given trunk road status.

The original concept of a ring road around the Manchester conurbation was, therefore, considered, by the Ministry, to be the responsibility of the local authorities. Later, however, it was accepted that the proposed Outer Ring Road would have trunk road status, with the Stretford-Eccles By-pass; this section of the M62 between Eccles and the Simister Interchange; and the Middleton Link; as its first elements.

M60 Motorway Junctions 18 to 19 *(Middleton Link, formerly part of M66)* - A contract for the construction of this Section of dual three-lane carriageway motorway was awarded by the NWRCU and work began in February 1973. It was completed and opened to traffic in August 1975. Route 9 in the Road Plan for Lancashire 1949 was described as 'tapping the industrial area of East Lancashire north of Manchester'.

It was intended to replace the A56 as far as the northern termination of the proposed Bury By-pass, it would follow the existing A56 Trunk Road to Edenfield, and then the A580 corridor to its junction with Route 8 near Whalley. Haslingden would be By-passed. Burnley and Blackburn traffic would connect with the Route at Edenfield and Haslingden respectively.

It was included within the category of 'Express (1st Group) Routes'. They would all have dual carriage-ways and almost 50% of the total length would be designed and constructed to 'motorway standard'. At its southern end, the first section of the Route was the one mile length of the proposed Middleton Link which subsequently, was to become part of the Manchester Outer Ring Road M60. From an interchange with the proposed Yorkshire Branch Road which later, was designated the Lancashire-Yorkshire Motorway M62, the Link extended in a south-easterly direction to a junction with the A576 at Higher Blackley.

M60 Motorway Junctions 19 to 24 - In June 1993 work on the first major contract began. The Denton-Middleton Section was opened to traffic in October 2000. This was 40 years after the completion in 1960 of the first Section, Stretford-Eccles By-pass.

In 1976 the firm of L G Mouchel & Partners, Consulting Engineers, was appointed to design the scheme for the long-awaited final section of the Manchester Outer Ring Road. Between December 1978 and August 1980 a Public Consultation exercise was carried out. Although a line had been protected by the local authorities in the area since the 1960's, several local variations were also submitted for consideration.

A Public Inquiry was held during 1986-87 and the line was finally determined in 1988. Following a further Public Inquiry in 1991-92 into the Side Road and Compulsory Purchase Orders, the statutory procedures were completed in 1993. The 10 mile section of motorway extends from the M67/M60/A57 interchange at Denton to the M60/A576 junction at Middleton. The route passes

through a wide variety of landscapes, much of it urban in character. There are four additional interchanges; at the A635 west of Ashton; A62 at Hollinwood; A663 Broadway; and a partial junction with the A664 Rochdale Road. The existing junctions at Denton and Middleton have been converted to full movement operation.

After considering various options, it was decided to separate the work into four major roadworks contracts and several large advance works contracts. The southern section of the route passes through one of three reservoirs at Audenshaw. To replace the water storage capacity lost to North West Water, a 20 mile long water main was laid in advance, from the Goyt Valley in Derbyshire to feed the remaining two reservoirs.

Left: Widening of Barton High Level Bridge in 1990. The M60 Motorway is seen where it crosses the Manchester Ship Canal between Junctions 10 and 11

Another significant water supply to the Manchester area is provided by a pipeline from Haweswater in the Lake District. The route of the Ring Road crosses this pipeline at several locations in the Moston/ Blackley/Audenshaw areas. Realigning the road to avoid it would have required the demolition of additional residential properties. It was decided, therefore, to divert the pipeline.

The route crosses four railway lines radiating from Manchester. One of these required an overbridge in the Ashton Moss area remote from public roads. It was possible to arrange access to the site for a separate contract to be completed before the roadworks contract started.

Two major drainage outfalls were laid in advance, the most significant being 2 miles in length, discharged into the River Medlock. The topography of the area and the profile of the motorway, in deep cutting, required a tunnel over half a mile long. In June 1993 work on the first major contract began. This involved the upgrading of the Middleton Link M66, which had been constructed in 1970/71 with dual two-lane carriageways, at the same time as the Lancashire Yorkshire Motorway M62.

The junction of the one mile length of M66 with the M62, was designed as a three level interchange. The M62 was to be at the top level, the M66 at the bottom level, and a roundabout with connecting slip roads at the mid level.

At the southern end of the Link, at the junction with Middleton Road, A576, a large roundabout was constructed. Provision was made for the M66 to be ultimately taken under it and extended to the south, as the first part of the north east quadrant of the Ring Road.

The 'upgrading' Contract included the substantial reconstruction of the Link, widening to provide dual four-lane carriageways, and a new bridge over the River Irk. The Contract was completed in February 1996. Meanwhile, in April 1995, work on the largest of the Contracts had begun. It involved the construction of a 4 mile length of motorway with dual three and four lane carriageways between the Denton Interchange and the River Medlock, within a contract period of three years.

The most unusual feature was the construction of the 1200 yard length of earth dam across the Audenshaw reservoir to replace that breached by the motorway. The site investigation had shown that there would be an adequate quantity of excavated clay available, to form the dense clay core of the dam. This was not forthcoming and severe delays occurred until suitable material was found beneath the floor of the redundant reservoir. Major lengths of permanent road diversion, link roads, and the construction of seven bridges was necessary, including a 400 feet long bridge over the Manchester-Leeds Canal and another of 360 feet over the Ashton Canal.

Also in 1995, a further Contract was awarded for various works on the remaining length of the project. In effect, an 'advanced contract', in that it involved the diversion and bridging of major radial road and rail routes serving Manchester. The task was further complicated by the need to maintain all traffic flows on these important commuting routes. It included a number of structures, for example, a bridge carrying the Manchester-Oldham railway over the line of the motorway, where the deck was placed during a 72 hour possession of the track. Close by, a new entrance had to be constructed, and platforms were moved at Hollinwood Station. It was also necessary to divert a length of the Rochdale Canal.

Before awarding the final Contract, to complete the motorway, the Highways Agency, acting on behalf of the Department of Transport, gave careful consideration to the form of contract. Concern had been expressed that, in carrying out the first three contracts, final costs and completion dates were overrunning. Among the various reasons for such a situation arising, was criticism of the '5th Edition' of the ICE Conditions of Contract, which had been used. It was decided, therefore, that a 'Design and Build' form of contract should be adopted, with 'quality assessment' of tenders.

As the successful tenderer, Balfour Beatty Major Projects became responsible for the design, supervision and construction of the works, within a set of agreed constraints. The firm appointed Gifford and Partners as their Designer, and Mouchel Consulting Ltd was appointed Employer's Agent, by the Highways Agency.

The Contract, which began in May 1998, has included the construction of 5 miles of dual two, three and four lane carriageways of the motorway between the River dual two, three and four lane carriageways of the motorway between the River Medlock and the Middleton Interchange, and the provision of eight bridges and 14 retaining walls. In the crossing of a 1 mile section of peat, at Blackley, a concrete piled raft was constructed. Piles were driven through the peat to a depth of 40 feet into the stiff clay below.

In early 1998, the whole of the Manchester Outer Ring Road, including the M63, sections of the M62, and the Middleton Link, M66, was renumbered M60. There are 27 junctions at an average spacing of 1.3 miles. A major programme of re-signing began in the Spring of that year, which included Compass Point signing for the various sectors. As well as strategic destinations, over 35 local destinations are signed at exits from the motorway.

The Denton-Middleton Section was opened to traffic in October 2000. This was 40 years after the completion in 1960 of the first Section, Stretford-Eccles By-pass. In comparison, the first 2 mile length of M25, the London Orbital Road, was opened in 1975 and the final section 11 years later in October 1986.

The M25 is 117 miles long compared with the 35 miles of the M60. Why should it have taken so long to complete the latter ? Has it been an example of the so-called 'North-South divide', in the allocation of financial resources?

M60 Motorway Junctions 24 to 27 *(Formerly M66 Portwood to Denton)* - The Contract was awarded in 1986 and work commenced between Brinnington and Denton in September 1986 an, on the other length, in January 1987. This Section of motorway was opened to traffic in April 1989. The 4 mile Portwood to Denton section of the Manchester Outer Ring Road, was the penultimate length to be constructed.

Left: Metrolink Bridge
At this point, near Junction 17,
M60 Motorway, roadbridge and
railway line pass one above the
other. A concrete girder bridge
was constructed directly above
the existing road from Heaton
Park to Whitefield, which itself
passes above the M60.

The firm of Parkman, Consulting Engineers, was appointed by the Department of Transport to undertake the design, and subsequent supervision of the construction.

Public Consultation into the proposals was held in February 1977. The only alternative put forward had been assessed previously, when it had been found that it did not have many of the advantages of the scheme under consideration.

A Public Inquiry was held in July 1982 and modifications, some of which were introduced to overcome objections, were considered at a further Public Inquiry in October 1985. The scheme involved the extension of the M63 from Portwood to Brinnington and the construction of a section of the M66 from Brinnington to Denton. At the time, that part of the Outer Ring Road on the eastern side of the conurbation, was numbered M66, as a southern extension of the Bury Easterly By-pass.

Following a favourable decision, a Contract was awarded in 1986 and work commenced between Brinnington and Denton in September 1986 and, on the other length, in January 1987. Apart from the completion of the interchange at Portwood and the building of bridges for the Denton Interchange, the Contract required the construction of Brinnington Interchange. This was to connect with, not only the A6017, Ashton Road, but also a By-pass of the A560. In addition it was designed to allow for the future connection of the proposed A6 (M), Stockport North-South By-pass.

A total of 16 bridges and two subways was required. The most significant, and spectacular, is the new Brinnington Railway Bridge which was designed, and the construction supervised, by British Rail. It was constructed alongside the track and moved into position during a weekend closure of the line. The Warren-girder steel bridge is the largest single span structure to be built by this method, to carry full British Rail traffic. Close by, a four span bridge was to be provided to carry the Lingard Lane/Brinnington Road over the motorway.

Over 3_ million cubic yards of excavation was carried out in cuttings, of which less than one third was used in the building of embankments, the majority of the remainder being utilised in landscaping treatment.

A section of the River Tame was diverted to a new alignment, and a large three span bridge was constructed to carry the motorway over the River. In the crossing of the River Goyt Valley, the River was diverted to the south, in order to improve the appearance of the area and simplify construction. The former course of the River was back filled.

The linked subways accommodated a diverted public footpath under the M63 and the A560 By-pass. It provided a main pedestrian route between the recreational areas within the two river valleys.

Major drainage works were required, including the construction of a 6 feet 6 inches diameter culvert

discharging into the diverted River Goyt, and tunnelling under Welkin Road. A twin 30 inch diameter inverted syphon carries a watercourse under the M66.

The complex nature of the project involved the construction of a combination of 2 mile lengths of both dual three-lane and dual two-lane carriageways of the motorway. In addition, 2 miles of all-purpose road and some 4 miles of link road were also required.

The Section of motorway was opened to traffic in April 1989.

This Technical Description was reproduced courtesy of the Motorway Archive Trust, with thanks to Harry Yeadon, past Lancashire County Surveyor and Bridgemaster, and Peter Hewitt. © The Motorway Archive Trust.

Below: Warren Bridge. Looking south from the pedestrian bridge east of Brinnington towards the junction at Bredbury. The empty middle section has been left in readiness for construction of the A6 (M) Stockport by-pass, which will provide a route from here to Hazel Grove along the Goyt valley. Ahead of us is the Warren (girder) bridge carrying the Manchester railway line.

Right: M60 and Tame Valley The M60 Motorway snakes down and then up over the River Tame to the east of Stockport. We are looking north from the pedestrian bridge to the east of Brinnington.

Photographic and Image Credits:

Stone Head, Abney Hall at Cheadle; M60 Junction 1 at dusk in the rain; The Blue Pyramid, looking west along the M60; The Blue Pyramid in fog – 2000; Stockport Railway Viaduct; Abney Hall Fish Pond; Steps at Abney Hall; Barnes Hospital; The Parsonage, Fletcher Moss, Didsbury; Palatine Road at Northenden; 'Rose Hill'; Sale Water Park New Bridge (2004); Sunset at Sale Water Park; Church of St Martin, Ashton-upon-Mersey; Trafford Centre, South west entrance; Trafford Centre, Griffins and Ladies; Trafford Centre Sunset; The Orient, Trafford Centre; Trafford Centre Barton Bridge; The Bridgwater Canal over the Manchester Ship Canal; Barton Aerodrome; A Panorama of Chat Moss; Worsley Delph; Worsley Green; Cobblestones on Bridgewater Canal Bridge; Wardley Hall; The River Irwell at Clifton; Pilkington Tiles at The Victoria Baths; Heaton Park Reservoir; Simister Church; Heaton Hall and Park; Heaton Park Folly; The Temple, Heaton Park; M60: Haulage Composite; Trafford Centre Container Terminal; Trafford Centre: Distribution Dépôt; Imperial War Museum North; The Imperial War Museum North; Sale Hall Dovecote; Abney Hall Owl Tower; Chadderton Mill; Gorse Mill; Gorton Monastery: An Angel for Adoption; Gorton Monastery Interior; Fairfield Moravian Settlement; Crime Lake, Daisy Nook; Allotments at Brinnington; Three Rivers: Goyt, Thame and Mersey; Stockport's Two Railway Viaducts; Motorcyclist, Barton High Level Bridge and the Trafford Centre; M60 at Junction 16; Metrolink Bridge; Blue Pyramid in the rain; Audenshaw Reservoir; M60 and Tame Valley; Warren Bridge; Railway to Manchester Airport; Barnes Hospital at Dusk; Pear Mill at Dusk: © Aidan O'Rourke 2004

Tombstone of James Watts II; Heaton Mersey Congregational Church; Harden Hall; Hyde Hall; Goyt Hall © M. Hyde 2004

Map of the M60 Motorway and of the Manchester Area at the endpapers; Map of pre-M60 numbering © AMCD (Publishers) Ltd. 2004 and © Ordnance Survey 2004

Himalayan Balsam; Nico Ditch, Denton Golf Course © AMCD (Publishers) Ltd. 2004

Sketch of Hannah Beswick and Dr White © Sarah Jane Stewart 2004

The Blue Pyramid under construction in 1991; Agecroft PFI Prison © Manchester Evening News

Art Treasures Exhibition 1857, Agecroft Hall, James Watts II, Alderman Fletcher Moss; Abney Hall 1857; Abney Hall Interior; Worsley New Hall; Aerial view of Prestwich Asylum; Aerial view of Barnes Hospital; Arrival by barge at Worsley New Hall ; Aerial view of Barnes Hospital; Barton Bridge © Manchester Central Library

Abney Hall - Drawing Room, Study and Agatha Christie; Stockport in the 1840s; © Stockport Libraries

Aerial View of Manchester Ship Canal; Barton High Level Bridge under Construction © Gordon McWilliams 2004

Agecroft Power Station © John Davies

Cradle of Shiloh © Salford Art Galleries

Aerial Views of Stockport in 1958; and 1982; and 1982 © Simmons Aerofilms 2004

Photographs 1-4 of Marple Hall © The Estate of Jack Wilkinson

Left: Barnes Hospital at Dusk. The clock tower of Barnes Hospital is eerily lit up at night, even though the building has long since been out of use. We are looking from Kingsway, close to the M60 motorway Junction 3 and slip road, which cut into the grounds of this former convalescent hospital.

Acknowledgements:

Photographs of Marple Hall by the late Jack Wilkinson. (For more of his photos visit the 'Virtual Tour' on the Marple Website at www.marple-uk.com).

Judith Smith, Greater Manchester County Bird Recorder, and Henry McGhie of the Manchester Museum for their advice on the effects of the M60 on local birdlife.

Nick Scarle, Manchester University Cartographic Unit, for the endpaper maps.

John Davies, for permission to reproduce his photograph of Agecroft power station.

Nora O'Rourke (née O'Connell), 5.10.1917 to 30.6.2004. Aidan's mum, who loved books.